Hanged for a Sheep

Crime and Punishment
in
Bygone Derbyshire

E. G. Power

You may as well be hanged for a sheep as a lamb - a saying dating back to the days when sheep stealing was punishable by death. If you stole a lamb you would be "hanged by the neck until you are dead." If you stole a sheep, you would get the same punishment, so you ran no greater risk in stealing the more valuable article.

Of course, there were other crimes besides stealing and other things stolen besides sheep! You will not find every kind of crime mentioned in this book, but it does tell you about some of the commoner crimes; about how the criminals were caught, and about the punishments they were given. In some ways, these things were very different in Derbyshire two hundred years ago, but in other ways you might think things haven't changed much!

Published 1981 by Scarthin Books Cromford Derbyshire
Phototypesetting and artwork by Prior to Print, 47 Friar Gate, Derby.
Printed by Heanor Gate Printing Limited, Heanor, Derbyshire.

ISBN 0 907758 002

Contents

Crime

CHAPTER ONE **Theft**
Stealing and carrying away — Temptation — Robbery — A case of sheep-stealing

CHAPTER TWO **Serious crime, murder and riot**
Felonious outrage — Bloody and Inhuman Murder — Tumults and Riotous Assemblies — The Reform Riots in Derby

Keeping Law and Order

CHAPTER THREE **Justices of the Peace and Parish Constables**
Do-it-yourself justice — Man traps and Spring guns — His Majesty's Justices of the Peace — Constables and Headboroughs

CHAPTER FOUR **The New Police**
Sobriety will be strictly enforced — A most unconstitutional force — Oil and wick for use of lanterns

Punishment

CHAPTER FIVE **Transportation and other punishments**
To be whipped at Derby — Hanged by the neck — Some of His Majesty's Plantations

CHAPTER SIX **Prisons**
The Hulks — The House of Correction — Straw for the prisoners — No Beer shall be admitted — A scrofulous and feeble subject

NOTES Derby Gaols — Escapes — Sources — Beaumaris Gaol — Books for further reading

CHAPTER ONE

Theft

Stealing and Carrying away

> **Jeremiah Hitchcock of Belper,** labourer, charged with feloniously stealing and carrying away eleven pears, of the value of one penny, on the 2nd of September 1830, out of the orchard of John Aldred, having before been convicted of a similar offence.

> This business was heard by Mr. Hurt and Mr. Strutt, and they adjudged him to be imprisoned three months in the House of Correction, and kept to hard labour.

Three months' imprisonment with hard labour for 'scrumping' eleven pears may seem a severe punishment to us, even if it was a second offence. The magistrates regarded it as a reasonable punishment however, and probably hoped that Jeremiah would be a reformed character after his stay in prison. Not so - a few months after his release he was in trouble again, in April 1831.

> **Jeremiah Hitchcock of Belper,** labourer, charged with feloniously stealing and carrying away 5 lbs. of steel, to the value of two shillings, the property of Thomas Swift of Belper, blacksmith.

This time, the magistrates thought that Hitchcock was becoming a hardened villain, the sort that England would be better off without.

> Hitchcock sent for trial at the Quarter Sessions at Chesterfield.

> Sentenced to be transported for seven years.

Whether Jeremiah Hitchcock was a hardened criminal or not we shall never know. He may have been just a poor labouring man who was tempted to steal because he had no money, and had a wife and children to keep. Certainly around two hundred years ago most people sentenced for stealing in Derbyshire were not professional thieves after valuable articles which they could sell for big money.

James Hogg of Crich, charged with entering a dwelling house and stealing certain wearing apparel, bread, butter, and eleven pairs of cotton stockings.

Transported for seven years.

Anthony Slater of Belper, framework knitter, charged with stealing one shirt, one shift, two handkerchiefs, one leather cap, two tablespoons and one teaspoon.

Transported for life.

John Hand, aged 13, of Ashbourne, charged with stealing one piece of bacon out of the shop of Samuel Walker at Ashbourne.

Sentenced to three months' imprisonment with hard labour, and to be once privately whipped.

Private whipping was done in the jail. It was considered more civilised than the public whippings which had been carried out in the Market Place in Derby and other towns earlier in the 18th Century.

Hugh Smith of Ripley, charged with stealing from the person of Joseph Fletcher of Ripley on Tuesday evening 25th October at Ripley Fair, a Half Crown.

Sentenced to two years' hard labour.

Joseph Smallwood and John Tugby both of **Willington,** labourers, charged with stealing and carrying away two dozen plates of the value of five shillings.

Sentenced to be transported for seven years.

These cases date from about 1760 to 1830 and are typical of hundreds of others. As you can see, this is very petty crime - the thieves were not likely to become very rich through stealing bread, butter, bacon, a teaspoon and other such stuff. In fact, it looks in some cases as if the main, or one of the main motives was hunger. They stole to eat, or to get something - anything - which could be easily and readily sold for a small amount of money. Almost anything would do, and the goods stolen in some cases make an odd assemblage. In 1794, for instance, a certain John Green, along with John Bean, broke into the house and shop of James Sims in Chesterfield, "betwixt 12 and 1 o'clock". John Green later confessed to stealing:

a man's shirt, a waistcoat, a pair of breeches, a piece of stuff to make a pair of breeches, a pair of stockings, a pair of money scales and weights, about two pounds of soap, two pounds of powdered sugar, one pound of raisins, and some other articles out of the shop which he cannot exactly remember."

County of Derby } The voluntary Examination & Confession of Joseph Smallwood taken before Us Two of his Majesty's Justices of the Peace for this County this 3 Day of Janry 1750 —

Who saith that on Saturday night last about Eight o'Clock, He in company with one John Tugby did upon Mr Greaves's behalf at Willington in this County, Cut open one Crate and took thereout about two Dozen of Cream Colour'd plates and about one Dozen of Cream Colour'd small Dishes, and laid them under a Hedge to lam all that night, on Sunday morning about Eight or Nine o'Clock they took the plates and Dishes and carried them to one Thomas Taylors a publican at Stanton by Swarkeston Bridge & Sold them to two Men who were in his House a Drinking, He says John Tugby Sold the plates and Dishes, but he cannot say for how much money, for that Jno. Tugby gave him only one Shilling

Taken the Day and year abovesaid before us
Fran: Ashby
J. Gisborne

His
Joseph X Smallwood
Mark

Joseph Smallwood confesses to stealing plates and dishes, for which he was later transported. A transcript appears in Chapter Five. Derbyshire County Record Office. *(Photo: Anthony Fisher).*

Not surprising! In fact, this John Green does not seem to have been very bright, as we can tell from the reason he gave for going to break into the house with John Bean. In his statement to the Mayor of Chesterfield, who was also a Justice of the Peace, Green said that he had only gone along because he (Bean) said they

> could pull the thatch off the house and that he (Green) might lay it upon another, so that it might not fall to the ground.

Yes, it does sound crazy, and we do not know what the Mayor of Chesterfield thought of the story! Perhaps John Green really did think that they were just going to "borrow" some thatch, which he could re-use on his own house. But that, of course, is how many rather simple-minded people still get themselves involved in criminal adventures which turn out to be much more serious than they first thought. Temptation is put in their way.

Temptation

Temptation was a real problem for household servants in the eighteenth and nineteenth centuries, when keeping a servant or a maid was much more common than it is today. Household servants were given their food and lodging, but they had to work very hard, get up before the family and go to bed last of all. They had little or no free time, and their pay was very low - a few pounds a year. At the same time, they were surrounded by the valuable ornaments, expensive jewellery and fine clothes belonging to their employers. If a servant girl got into debt or perhaps needed money to help her parents in a crisis, it would be very hard for her to resist the temptation to steal. Employers were aware of this and some would leave money lying around, apparently forgotten about, in order to test a servant's honesty. Even a normally honest person, however, might give in to temptation if she suddenly found that she needed money badly.

> **Elizabeth Strangeway, aged 18,** charged with stealing at Denby, a pair of pockets, a purse, an ivory case, a yard measure, two broaches, two small boxes, a muslin petticoat, a scarf, stockings and other articles, the property of John Barber, her master.
>
> To be imprisoned six months and kept to hard labour.

Derbyshire } The Examination of Robert Miles taken
to Wit } before me one of his Majestys Justices of
of the Peace for the s.d County this 30.th ~
Day of December 1742 ~ ~ ~ ~ ~

This Examinant saith that he was Born at Eccleshall in the
County of Stafford & is about the Age of 20 Years &
that he had lived with m.r Burton of Aston near
Sudbury in this County Three Years & a half soon after
which he hired himself to William Holles of Foston
and stay'd with him half a Year & then left the s.d
Servis about Three months since, and in which time
he has work'd Day Labour in the Neighbourhood but
since the Frost being out of business & having nothing
before Hand to support him. He Confeses that last
night betwixt Tenn & Eleven o'Clock he set a ladder up
to the Window of his late Masters Chees Chamber at his
House at Foston aforesaid & found the Casement of the s.d
Window open and put his hand into the s.d Chamber &
took out one Chees which he did Meerly for his present
Nessesity ~ ~ ~ ~ ~ ~ ~ ~ ~ ~ ~ ~

Taken before me the }
Day & Year aforesaid }

Statement made to J.P. in 1742 by Robert Miles, who stole a cheese "meerly for his present nessesity". Derbyshire County Record Office. *(Photo: Anthony Fisher)*.

Robbery

For ordinary stealing, the punishments, while severe by present day standards, were then considered mild, - seven years transportation, or a few months in jail. Robbing a person was thought to be much more serious than stealing from a house or a shop, and the recognised punishment was the death penalty, sometimes, but not always, commuted to transportation for life.

> **James Hawkesby, John Booth, Benjamin Taylor and William Taylor,** all of **Belper,** Nailers, charged with assaulting Benjamin Hides of Crich, framework knitter, putting him in bodily fear, and taking from his person four pounds, fourteen shillings, about 12 o'clock at night at Belper.
> Sent for trial at Assizes and sentenced to death. Afterwards transported for Life.

This was the most common kind of robbery about 200 years ago. There were those handsome, dashing highwaymen who held up stage coaches, and relieved the wealthy gentlemen of their cash, gold watches, etc., at the same time paying extravagant compliments to the lady passengers, but there were not many such gallant robbers about. If you travelled at night in Derbyshire, your experience of highway robbery would have been more like this, reported in the Derby Mercury, October 24, 1776.

> On Friday evening as Mr. Ready Ledwith, upholsterer in this town was returning home from a short ride he was stopped on the Osmaston Road about half a mile from hence by four footpads, one of whom held a pistol and another was armed with a long knife. They pulled him off his horse and saluted him with a volley of the most terrifying oaths, after which they robbed him of fourteen shillings but refused his watch which was a chased metal one.

Cautious robbers, because in those days watches were made individually and each one had the maker's name and its own number engraved on it, and this could be helpful in tracing the criminals.

Even these local Derby footpads can hardly have made a very good living by taking a few shillings now and then, so this kind of crime, like stealing,was also really associated with poverty, although no doubt they could have done an honest day's work instead, and would have been no worse off. We could hardly excuse them on grounds of hunger, or say that temptation had been put in their way. Most sheep-stealing cases involved both hunger and temptation, so it was no wonder that in spite of the death penalty sheep-stealing went on in the 17th and 18th centuries, all over Derbyshire, and in fact all over Britain.

A Case of Sheep Stealing

Two hundred or more years ago in Derbyshire to be poor meant the sort of poverty we now associate with famine victims in parts of Asia, Africa or South America. Poverty did not just mean being unable to afford a car, a colour television or a seaside holiday. It meant not eating, being cold for lack of clothes and fuel. The plight of the poor was worst in winter. It was a slack time for farming and a labourer might go for weeks without a day's work to be had. The weather was cold and wet, and a fire was needed to warm the room and to dry out wet clothes. Heavier, warmer colthes were needed. Hot meals would be very welcome, but with little or no money where were all these comforts to come from? Fresh meat was impossibly expensive in winter. Even the salted meat or fish, tasteless and stringy though it was, was too dear. The labouring poor lived, or existed, on bread, oatmeal porridge or oatcakes and very little else. Butter and cheese were luxuries.

To such people, not exactly starving, but desperate for meat, a sheep grazing on the hillside was not just a sheep. It was a set of sizzling lamb chops; a succulent mutton stew that you could gorge yourself on; a juicy leg of mutton that you could slice and slice again and suck the rich marrow from the bone, and take comfort from the memory of it for cold, miserable days and weeks afterwards.

A sheep was easily killed with a sharp knife. It was easy to cut up and carry home. The penalty if you were caught was death, but death from hunger and cold, or from disease caused by hunger and cold, was not unlikely anyway. So people took the risk.

One case of sheep-stealing in Derbyshire took place in 1693. We can piece the story together from faded yellowing documents in the Derbyshire County Archives, the statements made before a Justice of the Peace by the farmer whose sheep was stolen and by the people accused of the crime.

> The Information of **John Marshall of Greenfield** and **John Coates of Youlgreave** in the County of Derby taken upon oath before William Eyre, one of his Majesty's Justices of the Peace in and for the said County, upon the 13th day of December in the year of Our Lord 1693 . . . . .

> The Examination of **Robert Tompson** and **Elizabeth his sister** both of **Alport** in the County of Derby . . . . .

> The Examination of **William Tompson of Alport** aforesaid and his wife . . . .

Greenfields Farm, near Youlgreave. A typical 17th century farmhouse. The scene of sheep-stealing in 1693. *(photo: David Mitchell)*.

John Marshall was a farmer, living at Greenfield near Youlgreave. He kept sheep in an enclosure called Caslehurst. As it was not beside his house, he kept a check on it as often as he could. One cold Saturday morning early in December, he counted his sheep and one was missing,

a good wether sheep, stolen as he judges upon the Friday night.

Off he went to see his neighbour, John Coates. It was not the first time that either farmer had sheep stolen and they knew what to do. There was no use reporting the theft to the authorities. (There was no police force in 1693, anywhere in Britain). The only thing to do was to search any likely places and catch the thief themselves, before all the mutton was eaten and the fleece and bones hidden or buried. They would have to move quickly. The most they would have was a few days.

A few calls on likely families on Saturday and Sunday drew blanks. Time was running out. Enquiries on Monday produced no clues. By this time, there might be no evidence left, but both farmers, Marshall and Coates, were determined not to let the sheep-stealer get away with it. Taking a third man, probably a farm hand of Coates, with them, they tramped over to the hamlet of Alport, about a mile away, late on Monday night. . . . .

Robert Tompson and his sister Elizabeth were huddled over the dying embers of their fire. They were feeling well satisfied, having had more meat to eat in the last two days than they had had in the previous two months. And there was more to look forward to tomorrow, some ready cut up for the pot and a shoulder of mutton as well, covered with a cloth on a stool in the corner of the cottage. Then the knocking came on the door, and the shouts, "Open up!"

Robert and Elizabeth looked at each other, numb with horror. There was no time to hide the meat, and no place to hide it in their one-room cabin. Anyway, it would be better if it did not appear to have been deliberately hidden. They would just have to brazen it out.

The knocking on the door now turned to hammering and kicking so that if Robert had not unbarred it, it would have been smashed in in a few more seconds. As it swung open, in strode Marshall and Coates, hard-faced, accusing, the caked snow falling off their boots making dark wet patches on the earth floor. A quick look around the almost empty room and they soon set their eyes on the cloth over the stool in the corner. Without speaking, Marshall picked up the cloth and there was the mutton.

"How did you come by this?" asked Coates.

Elizabeth answered, because her brother stood silent, head hanging, as if he had already been condemned to death.

"I bought it at Bakewell market this morning, a hinder quarter and a shoulder of mutton."

Coates and Marshall looked at each other, without saying anything. This was the usual story. No farmer ever believed it, but as the meat was not hidden, perhaps this time the tale might just be true.

The two farmers knew what to do next. Marshall spoke to Robert Tompson,

"Your brother lives just across the way?"

Robert nodded.

"You two stay here!"

No sooner had Marshall and Coates gone out of the door than Robert and Elizabeth followed them, standing in the doorway and straining their eyes to see across the snow covered track to William Tompson's house. The sky was clouded and there was no moon, but the snow lying everywhere reflected what light there was. From a house further away a dog, disturbed by the noise, was barking continuously. At least, thought Elizabeth, William and his wife will have heard the banging on our door, and will have had time maybe, to hide their share of the mutton.

The door of the house opposite was already open, and Robert and Elizabeth saw Marshall and Coates go in, to be met by the Tompsons, husband and wife, hands spread out, protesting their innocence. But outside the open door there stood a third man, and, as Marshall and Coates came out after a few moments, this dark figure led them around the side of the house into the backyard.

Robert and Elizabeth had no time to think who this was or what it meant, before the two farmers and the third man reappeared, now carrying two black cooking pots. This was damaging evidence; William and his wife would have to make up some kind of excuse for the magistrate, to explain how two pots with meat and mutton fat in them came to be in the snow in their backyard.

Before William Eyre, the local Justice of the Peace, the next day the two different versions of the story were told. Marshall told how he and Coates had searched for stolen mutton and had found it first in Robert Tompson's house. Marshall and Coates then explained

> that they set a person to watch the house of William Tompson whilst they were searching Robert Tompson's house, and the person that watched saw William Tompson come out of his house and go into a yard on the backside of his house.

They found nothing inside the house but in the yard they found

> a black pot with mutton suet in it, newly thrown out of the window and another pott hidden in the snow

The four accused stuck to their story. Robert said

> he gave to his sister five shillings the Monday morning to bye meat at Bakewell.

Elizabeth insisted

> she bought that day a hinder quarter and a shoulder of mutton of a butcher in Bakewell.

What was the name of the butcher; what did he look like? asked the magistrate. His clerk recorded her lame reply.

> She can not tell the butcher's name nor what sort of man he was.

It was becoming more and more obvious that the mutton was stolen. As well as Elizabeth's inability to remember anything about the butcher who was supposed to have sold her the meat, it was most unlikely that she would have bought so much, two large joints, all at once. And it was also unlikely that her brother could have given her five shillings, as much as two or three weeks' wages, to buy meat.

However, what about William Tompson and his wife's story? They stated

> that she bought on Monday last a hind quarter of mutton of the same man that Robert Tompson's sister bought of, and likewise a pound and a half of suet.

How did the pot of suet come to be in the snow outside the window?

> She heard of a search made, and being afraid, she threw a pot with suet in it out of the window.

The magistrate considered carefully. There was still a faint possibility that the story was true. If a poor person had bought so much mutton, she would not want to risk its being found in a search. Some change of expression crossed the J. P.'s face as the clerk wrote down the explanation. If it was sympathy, the poor woman misinterpreted it and made a fatal mistake. She thought of a better explanation and, without stopping to think of the implications, stammered out that she wanted to alter her story. As the clerk dispassionately records

> Upon setting down her examination she denies that she threw it out, but that a dogg gott to it, and that was the occasion of its falling out of the window.

Her attempt to change the story, of course, cast even greater doubt on what was already almost unbelievable. It was much more likely that the Tompson brothers had stolen Marshall's sheep and had tried to hide the evidence when their houses were searched.

The four accused knew that no one would believe their tales of a sudden decision to buy an enormous quantity of mutton from an unknown and untraceable butcher in Bakewell. They need invent no more reasons for having two pots full of meat out in their back yard, in the snow in December. All the future held for them now was the assize courts and after that, the hangman.

In 1693 "hanged for a sheep" was literally true.

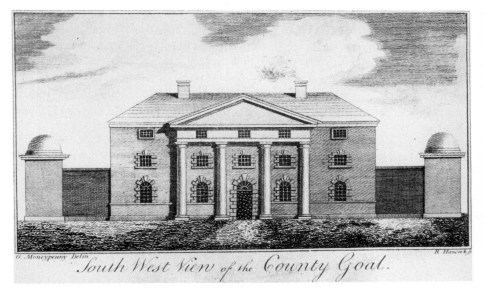

G. Moneypenny Delin.   *South West View of the County Goal.*   *R. Hancock fc*

The County Gaol built in 1756, in Friargate. Notice the common 18th century alternative of spelling gaol. Engraving in Derby Central Library, Local Studies Department. *(Photo: Anthony Fisher).*

Elebation of the New County Prison, Derby.

The County Gaol of 1827 in Vernon Street. The front has hardly changed since 1827, except for extra defences added after the Reform Bill Riots. Engraving in Derby Central Library, Local Studies Department. *(Photo: Anthony Fisher).*

CHAPTER TWO

Serious Crime, Murder and Riot

Felonious Outrage

> Whereas about half past 8 o'clock on Monday night, a most daring and felonious outrage was committed in Brook Street upon the person of Thomas Dawson, Engineer in the employ of Messrs. J & C. S. Peet. As he was returning from his employment, he was seized by a powerful and athletic man, who struck him violently on the head with some missile or heavy instrument which rendered him insensible for a considerable time.
>
> Whoever will give such information as shall lead to the conviction of the offender shall receive the Reward of Twenty Pounds from Messrs. J. & C. S. Peet.

This notice in the Derby Mercury in 1834 mentions one kind of felony. Felony, without going into a precise legal definition, meant any serious crime. Stealing, robbery, any attack on a person, damaging property, arson; all these were felonies, and convicts were often referred to as felons. The worst felony was treason against the Crown, but the most serious crime that courts normally had to deal with was murder. Up to 1828 these crimes carried the death penalty, so the principle, "you may as well be hanged for a sheep as a lamb", applied. If someone saw you setting fire to a stack of corn, for instance, there was a strong motive to kill the witness, if you could. You might then never be caught, and even if you were caught and convicted of murder, your punishment would be no worse than the punishment for arson, for which you would be hanged anyway. If you were lucky, sentence of death for lesser felonies than murder was sometimes commuted to transportation for life. This, however, was not a regular thing, and there was no way of telling whether the court would be merciful or not. In July 1817, ten men were tried and convicted in Derby.

> **John Brown, Thomas Jackson, George Booth and John King,** charged with setting fire to certain hay and corn stacks, the property of Winfield Halton, Esquire, of South Wingfield
>
> **John Wood and William Smith** for feloniously breaking into the dwelling house of George Astles at Hatton and stealing thereout various articles of apparel.
>
> **James Millar** for breaking into the dwelling house of William Trueman at Ilkeston and stealing sundry articles.
>
> **John Wain and Samuel Wain** for a burglary at Winster.
>
> **William Staples** for stealing a horse at Crich, the property of William Bunting.

All ten were sentenced to death but for six of them, the sentence was altered to transportation. The four arsonists were kept in jail, waiting.

> For some days after their condemnation, they cherished a hope that pardon or at least a mitigation of their sentence might be extended to them. Under this impression they persisted in asserting their innocence.

It was a vain hope. On Friday 15th August 1817 the four were hanged in front of the county jail in Derby. The Mercury reporter noted that they

> seemed but little affected by the sad solemnities by which they were surrounded

and recorded as a curiosity of human behaviour, that in the last few minutes before their execution three of the condemned men took shelter from a shower of rain.

> A heavy shower happening whilst the men were singing the hymn, two of them deliberately retreated to the shelter of an umbrella which was expanded on the drop, and a third placed himself under cover of the doorway.

Bloody and Inhuman Murder

Assault and arson leads us on to murder, which has always had, and still has, a fascination for even the most law-abiding citizens. Nowadays, the stories of great robbers, spies, and frauds are featured prominently in the Sunday papers and we read the accounts of murders avidly. We follow trials reported in the media, and discuss the weight of evidence for or against the accused, and pass comment on the justice or otherwise of the sentence as it seems to us. If there are not enough real murder cases to satisfy us, we read fictional whodunnits, or watch murder and detection series on T.V.

Two hundred years ago, our forefathers were just as eager to hear the gruesome details of a murder and to condemn or exonerate the murderer as they saw fit. Most murderers, if one can generalise, were willing, not to say eager, to justify their action, or at least to explain it in such a way as not to appear too inhuman and heartless.

Every condemned murderer told his own version of his story to some lucky printer, who published it in the form of a broadsheet or pamphlet, which then sold like hot cakes to the crowd at the execution. No doubt part of the interest was in the fact that you could read the life story and the details of the crime, and actually be present in person for the final act in the drama.

These "dying confessions" of convicted murderers follow a kind of general pattern. Whether this pattern was always observed by the murderer, or imposed on the story by the printer, is impossible to tell, for obvious reasons. At any rate, the public seemed to like a moral tale so the murderer's life usually began with a respectable birth; then in childhood a neglect of sound parental advice; an association with evil companions; neglect of religion, etc. and then inevitably, the murder, followed by capture and retribution. (Many crimes of murder went unsolved but they, of course, did not give rise to "dying confessions" of this sort).

This pattern is followed in one such confession printed in Derby in 1776. The title, as was usual, is almost a summary of the story in itself.

The Life, Tryal, Behaviour, Confession and last Dying words of **Matthew Cocklane,** alias **Coghlan,** who was executed on Derby Gallows on Thursday the 21st Day of March 1776 for the barbarous, cruel, bloody and inhuman Murder of Mrs. Mary Vickars at her house in Derby, which he perpetrated in the night betwixt Sunday the 18th and Monday the 19th Days of December 1774.

I, Matthew Cocklane, am now in the Thirty first Year of my age, was born in the town of Carlow in the Kingdom of Ireland of creditable Parents. My father followed the trade of a Tanner.

I was sent to school at an early age but I gave little heed to instruction and when arrived at the age of nine or ten years, frequently absented myself from school for weeks together.

At the age of 13 I enlisted into the 33rd Regiment and continued in it about ten years.

Matthew then settled in Derby, married, and worked in the iron and copper works. Then he fell into bad company.

I having got acquainted with a young fellow, one George Foster, this young man advised me frequently to commit things repugnant to civil society. He begged me to go along with him and that I should not want for money.

Matthew knew a girl in Derby who had worked for a rich widow, Mrs. Vickars. The girl told him that Mrs. Vickars never kept more than one servant and always had a large amount of money in her house.

Matthew Cocklane and George Foster made a plan to rob the old lady and fixed on Sunday night 18th December. George hung about watching the house, and Matthew met him after finishing work at the copper mills at midnight. Matthew had an iron bar with him, or as he called it in his story, an iron pin. Matthew got in through a window at the back of the house and then opened the front door to let in George

We immediately rushed upstairs. I told him to take off Mrs. Vickars whilst I went and searched for the money. Mrs. Vickars jumping out of bed with a great deal of vigour I immediately knocked her down with the iron pin. This not stopping the noise that she made my companion immediately seized on her and got her down behind the door.

While George was keeping Mrs. Vickars from shouting for help, Matthew broke open the lid of the money chest in the bedroom and took out several purses. Just then, Mrs. Vickars' maid appeared at the doorway, having come down from her attic room to see what the noise was.

I told her to go upstairs or I would take her life that minute.

This was later to prove a fatal mistake for Matthew, but it was an effective threat, for the maid ran back upstairs. However, this was not the only interruption. It was a week before Christmas, and there were various parties and celebrations taking place, late at night. The town band was returning from one of these and happened to pass the house just as the maid ran back upstairs.

> At that instant the Town Waits or Town music were passing by Mrs. Vickars' house. This alarmed me. I went downstairs, thinking that my companion had only stopped Mrs. Vickars' mouth with a handkerchief.

The two thieves went by different ways to Nun's Green, then on the outskirts of Derby, and found when they counted the money that they had about £300 between them.

> We then settled it for me to go Leek Road and he to go by Chester for Liverpool and to meet there. I did not know Mrs. Vickars was dead. The first information I had of it was from a handbill which was read in my hearing at a public house at Liverpool. On my companion's arrival, I asked him if it was true. He told me he believed she was dead but it did not signify, for he had got three gold rings from her fingers.

The two murderers then took ship to Ireland. There they tried their hand at highway robbery which they bungled. George Foster was shot and died three days later, and Matthew Cocklane was captured and brought back to Derby to stand trial.

He thought he had a very good chance of getting off. No one had seen him breaking into, or leaving, Mrs. Vickars' house on the night of the murder. He had not taken any jewellery which could be proved to have belonged to Mrs. Vickars. The maid had not seen his face in the dark, and could not swear that she recognised him as one of the robbers in her employer's bedroom. But she had heard a voice saying, "Go back upstairs or I'll take your life this minute." And she testified that it was Matthew Cocklane's voice.

This was enough for the jury, and Matthew was condemned to death. Later, of course, he confessed and told the whole story. He was hanged in Derby on 21st March 1776. There is a brief description of his execution in Chapter Five.

Tumults and Riotous Assemblies

If murder fascinates us because it is such a personal crime, riot was the crime which the authorities feared most, two hundred years ago, and with good reason.

Rioting, for a variety of reasons and with varying degrees of severity, was quite common during the 18th century and it became a worse problem during the early years of the 19th century. There had always been food riots, because of scarcity and high prices, for which merchants and dealers were blamed and attacked. There had always been the likelihood of riots at election times, even though, or perhaps because most people were not allowed to vote. Religious riots still occurred in the 18th century, often against the open air preaching of John Wesley, the mob encouraged by the supporters of the Established Church of England. The worst religious riots in the 18th century were the Gordon Riots in London in 1780. These were sparked off by the old cry of 'No Popery', and were led by the eccentric Lord George Gordon. The mob had a free hand for four days; four prisons were broken open, Roman Catholic churches were destroyed and, as usual, shops and liquor stores were looted. Troops eventually restored order.

To these kinds of riots others were added in the late 18th and early 19th centuries. Enclosure, the re-arrangement of arable and common grazing land, village by village, let to rioting in some places. The setting up of toll gates on the roads caused riots, as, for instance in the Bristol area. The decline of some industries and the rapid development of others; low wages and high prices, with the authorities and employers frowning on early attempts to organise trade unions; these also gave rise to riots, disturbances and outrages, as for example in the East Midlands in the early 1800's.

To deal with riots, the authorities had very few resources; in rural areas, the parish constable; in towns, a handful of watchmen. There is more about watchmen and parish constables in Chapter Three. If trouble was anticipated, special constables could be sworn in, recruited from the law abiding population. These were usually ineffective as they had no training or instruction. The only effective way to deal with a riot was to call for troops, and by the time these arrived on the scene the mob had usually had two or three days to themselves.

The handling of riots was based on the Riot Act of 1715. Before this Act, rioters might be charged with theft, damage to property, arson, or whatever, and in serious riots the charge could be treason. The Riot

Act of 1715 created a separate offence of rioting. If twelve or more people, riotously assembled, did not disperse, a magistrate was to read the official proclamation telling them

> to disperse themselves and peaceably to depart to their homes or to their lawful businesses, upon the pains and penalties contained in the Act made in the reign of King George I for preventing tumults and riotous assemblies. God Save the King!

The rioters were given an hour to disperse. Those who were still there after the hour was up were automatically guilty of riotous assembly, and could take no legal action against the authorities if they were injured while being forcibly dispersed. The Act did not in fact require magistrates to wait for an hour before trying to disperse the crowd, but most magistrates interpreted in that way.

The Reform Riots in Derby

The riots in Derby in October 1831 had many features in common with other riots two hundred years ago. The cause was political. The House of Commons has passed a Bill to give more people the right to vote, and this had widespread support throughout the country. The House of Lords rejected the Bill, which at that time meant the end of it. This caused great disappointment and in the next few days there were serious riots in many towns, particularly in Bristol and Nottingham, where the castle was burnt down.

In Derby the news of the killing of the Reform Bill by the House of Lords came with the arrival of the London coach about seven o'clock on Saturday evening, 8th October 1831. A small crowd was already waiting to hear the news when the coach arrived, and they decided to mark the death of the Reform Bill by tolling the bell of All Saints Church. They forced the vicar to give them the keys of the church, and within an hour or so the bells of All Saints, St. Alkmunds and St. Peters were all tolling in a very ragged but enthusiastic fashion. About ten o'clock, according to the Derby Mercury reporter

> the concourse of persons in the market place became alarming and exhibited considerable excitement.

In the Cornmarket stood the house and shop of Mr. William Bemrose, who had been an outspoken critic of the Reform Bill, and this was an obvious target for the mob. Bemrose sold books, music and instruments, and he had an apprentice called Henry Morley who later gave evidence about the attack.

Henry Morley heard and saw the crowd in the Market Place and Corn Market and told Mrs. Bemrose, whose husband was away, that they were coming to attack the shop. They began throwing stones at the upstairs windows, (the lower windows were shuttered) and in ten or fifteen minutes all but three panes of glass had been smashed. This was only the beginning of a night of terror for Henry Morley and Mrs. Bemrose.

Some time after one o'clock in the morning the mob came back, throwing stones at what was left of the windows, at the shutters, and at the shop sign. About three o'clock, they came back again and smashed holes in the wooden shutters with iron bars. Henry watched and saw men's arms come through the holes, reaching down to snatch anything in the shop window.

At half past four, the rioters were back again. This time, they finished off the window shutters and smashed in the shop door. About twenty men surged in and began to throw books, paper, and musical instruments about. Some carried the goods out; others threw them through the window into the street where parties of rioters passing by carried them off or kicked and stamped on them. Boys ripped sets of pages out of the books, tore the paper up and threw it up in the air in handfuls. The noise of splintering wood, smashing of musical instruments and shouting from inside the shop and in the street was deafening. As dawn began to break, the mob went away, one man saying to Henry Morley who had watched, helpless

We'll go now, and come again at night and finish him up.

Sunday morning dawned on scenes of destruction all around Derby. The mob which had gathered in the Market Place had not confined its attention to Bemrose's shop. The rioters had split up into several groups, some large, some small, and every well-known opponent of the Reform Bill in the district had received their unpleasant attentions. These included Thomas Cox's house in Friargate, Markeaton Hall and Chaddesden Hall, the home of Henry Sacheverell Wilmot. There the mob began

to demolish, pull down and destroy the dwelling house, stable, coach-house and outhouses.

Elsewhere in the town, street lamps and windows were broken, and shops were looted. A few rioters were arrested and taken to the Borough Gaol. The Mayor and town council and law abiding citizens were in the state of fear and desperation usual in a town gripped by riots. The Mayor called a public meeting in the Town Hall in the Market Place at nine o'clock on Sunday morning, 9th October, to see if anything could be done to restore order.

Some of the rioters demanded that three people arrested and jailed the previous night should be released. When the Mayor refused, their answer was

> they would be damned if they would not go and break open the prision

and they did.

Fourteen or fifteen hundred men and women marched off to the Borough Gaol at No. 45-51 Friargate, equipping themselves with an uprooted cast-iron lamp post as they went. Ralph Wibberley, the turnkey, heard the noise of the mob coming and fastened the outer door, but when he saw the size and the mood of the crowd, he advised the governor to give in to their demands. So the rioters of the previous night were let out and hoisted on to their comrades' shoulders, with tremendous cheers.

This measure of success did not satisfy the mob, who proceeded to smash the doors in, using the iron lamp post as a battering ram. In a few minutes, they were inside, and let all the convicts out, totalling twenty-three people. This encouraged the mob to try for greater things. Shouting, swearing, and yelling "Reform", they soon took up the cry, "To the County Gaol!" and surged on, sweeping innocent townspeople along with them in the crush.

At the County Gaol in Vernon Street the governor appeared and told them to disperse, only to be answered with curses and a shower of stones. In reply to this, armed guards appeared on the wall. This provoked the cry

> Damm you, we will be at you soon, and fetch those devils down from above.

The governor gave the order to fire and several shots cooled the rioters' enthusiasm, although no one was seriously injured except one young man who was shot in the stomach. This was John Garner, aged 17. The Derby Mercury reported, sadly, as we are too often accustomed to nowadays

> It is believed that this young man possessed a good character and had taken no share in the proceedings.

John Garner died the next day.

At about half past five on Sunday afternoon the soldiers which the magistrates had requested arrived at last from Nottingham. They were a troop of the 15th Hussars. Their presence deterred further violence in the centre of Derby on Sunday evening, and they patrolled the main

27

streets all night, along with the special constables who had been enrolled. This prevented any major trouble during the night but there were still small groups of rioters and looters roaming the town.

On Monday, 10th October, people again began to gather in the Market Place, some intent on trouble, some wanting to demonstrate their support for Reform, some simply to see what would happen. The authorities had decided to make arrangements so that people could sign a massive petition to the king in favour of Reform, and stalls for the signing of the petition were set up in the Market Place. This, however, seemed too tame a conclusion to the excitements of the last few days for some people, and as the workmen set up the stalls they pulled them down and smashed them up.

The magistrates decided reluctantly to take the final step. They read the Riot Act, and requested the military commander to clear the Market Place. After the usual hour's delay, the cavalry moved forward, sabres drawn, carbines ready to fire if necessary. By this time, most of the crowd packed in the Market Place were trying to leave, but of course the escape routes were narrow and there were still more people coming in to the town centre to see what was happening. One of these was Josiah Shepherd of Sawley, who was with a friend, Mr. Berry of Queen Street, Derby. Later in evidence he told his story.

> He was with Mr. Berry on Monday, 10th October, went towards the Market Place. A soldier came riding up. Berry said, "We must return they are clearing the Market Place." As we were returning a shot was fired. The ball passed through my hat and struck a man who was on the pavement about two yards distant from me. I did not at first know what had happened to my hat. I turned to look and saw the man down. I heard him groan and saw him bleeding.

A very lucky escape for Josiah Shepherd and an unlucky accident for John Hickin who just happened to be in the way of the bullet. This was the second death. A third was that of Henry Haden, who died after being injured in the crush. The crowd was dispersed, fortunately without any more serious injuries, and over the next few days order was restored. Yeomanry from Radbourn, Burton-on-Trent and Leicestershire arrived to assist the Hussars. (Yeomanry were volunteer part-time cavalry, mounted and equipped largely at their own expense). Several thousands of pounds' worth of damage had been caused when the council and citizens took stock of the situation. The thought in most people's minds was that it could have been much worse. A few years later when the question was mooted of having a proper police force for Derby, people remembered the Reform Riots of 1831.

CHAPTER THREE

J. P.s and Parish Constables

Do-it-yourself Justice

About 200 years ago, our ancestors' expectations of what the government should do for them were lower than they are today. The state was then much less involved in the everyday lives of citizens. In maintaining law and order, which along with defence, was its main function, the state merely established the framework of a system. The subjects of the state were expected to make the system work themselves. The system of preventing crime and apprehending criminals involved an enormous voluntary effort - paid officials were rare. If people were not satisfied with the unpaid J. P.s and parish constables on whom most of the work fell, then they could and did take steps themselves, with the approval of the state but without any actual help from it. One way of doing-it-yourself was to offer a reward for the capture of a thief:

A Robbery

Chesterfield, March 14, 1799

Whereas on Sunday Night last the 10th inst. between the Hours of nine and eleven o'clock, a Bag containing 34 Dozens of BROWN COTTON HOSE directed to Messrs. **S. Unwin & Co., Sutton,** was stolen out of a Stage Waggon in Holywell Street, Chesterfield, belonging to Mr. John Thompson, Carrier, of the same Place. - Whoever will give information to the said Mr. Thompson of the Person or Persons who committed the said Robbery, so that he, she or they may be fully convicted thereof shall receive a Reward of

TWENTY GUINEAS

If more than one were concerned in the said Robbery, and an Accomplice will impeach his Accomplice or Accomplices, so that he, she or they may be convicted, he shall receive the same reward of Twenty Guineas, and every endeavour will be made to obtain his free pardon.

JOHN THOMPSON

These cotton stockings were the 18th century equivalent of the goods that nowadays "fell off the back of a lorry".

John Thompson, a well-established carrier, could offer a sizable reward. Private persons offered smaller rewards for the arrest of a thief.

BURGLARY

Whereas early on Sunday morning last, some person or persons broke into the dwelling house of John Spencer at Etwall in the county of Derby, and stole thereout a purse containing three sovereigns and a half, a silver watch, maker's name "Reeves, Lamberdhurst, No. 3947", a penknife, twopence-halfpenny in copper, a shirt, a pair of stockings and other articles.

Two sovereigns reward will be paid by the said John Spencer, on the apprehension and conviction of the offender, or offenders, over and above the reward allowed by the Etwall Association for the Prosecution of Felons.

This notice from the Derby Mercury of 21st March 1832 mentions another way of supplementing the work of the parish constables, the do-it-yourself-together-with-other-people method, or the Association for the Prosecution of Felons.

Around 200 years ago almost every town or district had such an Association. Anyone could belong to it, on payment of a fee. In practice, it was the wealthier members of the community who formed these Associations, the purpose of which was to pay set rewards for information on a whole range of crimes, and in this way, to make detection and punishment more likely. The Belper Association for the Prosecution of Felons offered five guineas reward in cases of murder, burglary, highway robbery, horse-stealing and arson; three guineas for information in connection with the theft of other livestock, and smaller rewards for lesser offences down to half a guinea in cases of

"unlawfully interfering with dams or fishing therein."

During the wars between Britain and France, 1793-1815, following the French Revolution in 1789, other Associations were formed in Derbyshire, as in other counties. There were certain political groups advocating changes in the British system of government, ranging from those who wanted a Republic to those who merely wanted more people to be given the right to vote. In the atmosphere of wartime, all these tended to be branded as traitors by those who supported the Establishment. Loyal Associations were formed, to counteract, in the words of the Loyal Association of Belper:

the pernicious Opinions which have of late been industriously circulated by Pamphlets, and otherwise propagated by certain Clubs..

The members resolved

to support the Authority of the King and the Laws, to resist all Violations of the public Peace, and to maintain good Order and Tranquillity.

And they promised to do all they could

to bring to Punishment all such who shall distribute or expose to the public Eye, any Pamphlet or Papers, containing Opinions or Sentiments, tending to promote disaffection, and encourage Sedition or Innovation.

According to the Derby Mercury

These Resolutions were carried into the Market Place and signed by nearly three hundred Persons. And the Evening was spent with the utmost conviviality.

Rewards offered by people who had their property stolen, and funds set up to pay the cost of bringing thieves and other offenders to justice - these were two ways of applying the D.I.Y. principle to the suppression of crime. Another way was even more extreme. This was to provide not just the means of detection and prosecution on a private basis, but instant punishment for the offender as well! The people who suffered from this two hundred years ago were poachers.

Mantrap. The effect can be seen in the Chapter heading woodcut! *(Photo: University of Reading, Institute of Agricultural History and Museum of English Rural Life).*

Man traps and Spring guns

The heyday of poaching was from about 1770 to 1830, although there had been poachers about long before that, and it is still going on today. Small scale poaching is one of those crimes like minor smuggling, which the law makes a crime, and which many people can see no particular harm in, really.

The laws which dealt with poaching were called the Game Laws, and they were very strict about who was allowed to "take game". Only landowners and their eldest sons, and their regular gamekeepers could shoot game. No one else could; not even a rich farmer who rented land but did not actually own it himself.

GAME

Whereas the game in the Manor and Liberty of Belper has been much destroyed by poachers and unqualified persons, Notice is hereby given that men are employed to watch and detect those found with dogs, guns, etc. and every person so found after this notice will be proceeded against according to law.

This notice was put in the Derbyshire Chronicle and Universal Weekly Advertiser by Paul Jodrell, Lord of the Manor of Belper. "Unqualified persons" meant anyone except Paul Jodrell, his eldest son, and his gamekeepers.

As a deterrent and an instant punishment for poachers, many landowners in Derbyshire and elsewhere set man-traps and spring guns.

SPRING GUNS

Notice is hereby given that Spring Guns are set in the woods, plantations and coverts in Alderwasley, in the county of Derby. Any person found trespassing, on any pretence, after this public notice will be prosecuted.

The notice might have read "will be prosecuted if he survives" because an encounter with a spring gun could well be fatal. The gun, loaded with shot, was fixed in a tree. A wire was set across the path below. a few inches above the ground. The wire led to the trigger of the gun. Anyone whose foot caught in the wire set the gun off, and he got a full charge of shot at close range.

The other kind of instant punishment was the man trap. Man traps had huge steel jaws, sometimes serrated, which were worked by a very powerful spring. The jaws opened on either side of a metal plate, The trap was placed flat on the ground and hidden with a few twigs or fronds of bracken. A suitable place was on a narrow path, or at a gap in a hedge or fence where a poacher was likely to step through. When he put his foot on the plate, Bang! the jaws slammed together on his leg. This might actually break his leg, and it would certainly hold him fast until the gamekeepers came round in the morning. To make sure there was no escape, the man trap was usually fixed by a chain to a tree or a stout stake.

Like spring guns, man traps did not distinguish between poachers and other people - boys birdnesting, children picking wild flowers or blackberries, even forgetful gamekeepers! There were so many nasty accidents, in fact, that Parliament made spring guns and man traps illegal in 1827, and poachers had to be caught and brought to justice like any other criminal. This duty fell on the parish constables and the Justices of the Peace.

VAN DIEMAN'S LAND

Bebbington, Printer, 22, Goulden St. Oldham Road Manchester
and sold by H. Andrews, 27, St. Peter Street, Leeds.

Come all you gallant poachers, that ramble void of care,
That walk out on a moonlight night, with your dog, gun, and
  snare;
The hare and lofty pheasant you have at your command,
Not thinking of your last career upon Van Dieman's Land.

Poor Thomas Brown, of Nottingham, Jack Williams, and Poor
  Joe,
Were three determin'd poachers, as the country well doth know
At night they were trepann'd by the keepers hid in sand,
And fourteen years transported were upon Van Dieman's Land

The first day we landed upon the fatal shore,
The planters came around us—their might be 20 score,
They rank'd us up like horses and sold us out of hand, (Land.
They yok'd us in a plough, brave boys, to plough Van Dieman's

Our cottages we live in are built of clods and clay,
And rotten straw for bedding, yet we dare not say nay,
Around our cots a curling fire--we slumber when we can,
And drive the wolves and tigers oft upon Van Dieman's Land.

Oft times when I do slumber, I have a pleasant dream,
With my sweet girl sitting near me close by a purling stream
Thro' England I've been roaming, with her at my command,
And waken broken-hearted upon Van Dieman's Land.

A poaching ballad of the early 19th century, which fits the tune of The Lincolnshire Poacher.
Van Diemen's Land was the name used for Tasmania up to 1825.

His Majesty's Justices of the Peace

The J. P.s or magistrates of Derbyshire, or any other county, also conformed to the do-it-yourself principle. In effect, the state said to the gentry of each county, "run your own county affairs". The state selected wealthy landowners, gave them the respected title of Justice of the Peace, provided them with a framework of procedure and the power to levy rates, and then let them get on with it. The J. P.s were not, of course, paid for carrying out their duties, but it was a great honour, and a responsibility which the gentry felt they were bound to accept.

The county J. P.s undertook a great many activities which would nowadays be organised by the County Council or District Councils. They saw to the repair of roads and bridges; they issued licences for alehouses and kept a record of authorised gamekeepers. They also looked after the County Gaol. Individually, they heard and recorded statements, complaints and confessions, and investigated breaches of the peace. As we saw in Chapter Two, they might be required to deal with riots and tumults. In pairs usually, they held Petty Session courts every week or so, in the main towns in Derbyshire, and dealt out summary justice to petty thieves, poachers and beggars.

Four times a year, most of the J. P.s met for Quarter Sessions, where all kinds of County business was discussed and settled, and more serious offences were tried. In some cases, the accused persons were ordered to the gaol, to await trial at a later date by the judges of the Assize Courts, who made a yearly circuit around different parts of England hearing and deciding the most important cases.

Constables and Headboroughs

A J. P. could not, of course, maintain law and order, or the King's Peace, as the 18th Century put it, without help. He could not be every-where at once. His duty was mainly not to do the job but to see that the job was done. The men in the front line were the Parish constables - one, two, or sometimes more, in each parish. They were also called Petty Constables or, in some districts, Headboroughs. In the 18th and early 19th centuries, the Parish Constable was not at all like the later Victorian village constable or village bobby to whom many elderly people look back with affection.

The Parish Constable of 200 years ago, like the J. P., was unpaid, a volunteer. He was untrained, and was not provided with any uniform or equipment. He could claim expenses for travelling to apprehend a suspect or for attending at court, and no doubt he made sure that his claim fully covered his expenditure. But no one got rich by being a parish constable.

The duty of this unpaid parish constable, or headborough, was to arrest criminals, search for stolen goods and generally "keep the peace". As he had his own living to make, he could not spend his days and nights patrolling the village and the countryside. He carried on with his farming, shopkeeping, blacksmithing, or whatever, until someone went to him for help. Then he led the search, or the chase, or, on rare ocasions, might do a bit of elementary detection, as in the following early case. The evidence was given by

> **John Dodge of Smithsby** in the county of Derby, husband, (= farmer) taken upon his corporall oath before James Abney Esq. the fourth day of January Ann. Dom. 1650

(It is worthwhile comparing this case with that of the Thompsons in Chapter One).

John Dodge said that

> he and others found one of his sheep's skins with a paunch (= entrails) in Smithsby windmill close, from whence they followed a track of a man's feet in the snow very near to Robert Stevenson's house.

This, of course, did not prove to James Abney, J. P., that Stevenson had stolen the sheep. But there was more evidence. With the constable of Ashby they had searched Stevenson's house and found

> all the bones of a raw shoulder of mutton together with a little knife which had wool sticking upon it.

So how was Stevenson to explain that to the J. P.? Not very convincingly, like this

> He bought the said shoulder of mutton, the bones whereof were found. . . . . of a butcher which stood in Ashby street to sell meat on Tuesday last, being New Years eve, but his name he knoweth not.

Almost enough to convince the J. P. of Stevenson's guilt, but the constable of Ashby had some more evidence to clinch the matter. He had examined carefully the footprints in the snow and he had also examined Robert Stevenson's shoes and by studying

> the length, breadth and patches of the said Stevenson's shoes did declare the said marks to be made by the said Stevenson's feet.

How many detectives in fiction solved their crimes by examining footprints! But this was in 1650, and done by a humble parish constable.

Occasionally a parish constable might stumble upon evidence which he was not expecting! William Persivall of Haywood in the Parish of Bakewell informed a J. P. of how one of his master's turkeycocks was missing, and he went

> with the assistance of Edward Padley, headborough of the Hamlett of Abney in the Township of Eyam to search for the same at divers and sundry houses, and (amongst the rest) at the house of **Henry Brushfield of Nether Padley,** labourer. And upon search in a private place over a parlour in the said house he found, not the said turkey cock which he sought for, but did then and there find three hinder quarters and part of a forequarter of mutton, ... but how it came thither he knows not.

It must be said that not all parish constables in Derbyshire in the 18th century were as keen as the constable of Ashby nor as lucky as Edward Padley. It was often difficult to find suitable men, and in places where there was little crime, the people of the parish often managed without a constable at all. A report to the Derbyshire J. P.s in 1828 complained that

> it is certainly the case that a large number of Townships in Derbyshire, perhaps about one-fifth of the whole, are, and have been for many years destitute of a responsible and legally appointed Constable.

The system of unpaid and often unwilling parish constables seems to have worked reasonably well up to about the middle of the 18th century. In those times, the population of a village was very small, everybody knew everybody else, there were certain recognised ne'er-do-wells, and any stranger in the community was noticed straight away, and watched.

In the early 19th century, however, populations were increasing. Families moved from place to place more frequently, as jobs became available in new factories, mines, and on the railways. It was much harder for a parish constable to keep track of all his "clients".

As well as this, the kind of jobs people did were different. In the 18th century, most constables were farmers or self-employed men in trades like blacksmith, wheelwright or grocer. They could leave what they were doing if called upon to search for stolen mutton, or break up a fight. As the 19th century went on, more and more suitable men were wage earners, whose employer would not be over-pleased if they went off from work at short notice to deal with a crime. We can see some examples of these from lists of parish constables made between 1865 and 1868:

Parish	Occupation of constable
Darley Abbey	overlooker (in cotton mill)
Linton	machine man
Long Eaton	engine man
Chaddesden	pointsman

None of these could easily carry out the duties of Parish constable. For several reasons, then, the old system of parish constables had to end, and be replaced by a system suited to the conditions of the more crowded industrial age.

Truncheons and handcuffs in Derbyshire Police Museum, Butterley Hall, Ripley. Truncheons, Top to Bottom: Edwardian Horse staff. Victorian riot stick. 1950 standard issue. 1859 Derbyshire Constabulary. Ripley and Staveley special constables' issue. 1860 Chesterfield painted staff. 1950 Policewoman's staff. Handcuffs, Left to Right: 1850's standard issue. Modern design. Apprentice handcuffs. *(Photo: Anthony Fisher)*.

CHAPTER FOUR

The New Police

Sobriety will be strictly enforced

The extremes of wealth and poverty found in large towns and cities; the crowds in which a pickpocket can work and into which a thief can disappear; the continuous arrivals and departures of tourists, visitors, businessmen and other travellers; these things have always meant a greater crime problem in cities than in the countryside. London was by far the largest city in England in the early 19th century, so the problem of crime was greatest there, and so it is not surprising that the first attempt to improve on the old parish constable system of policing was made in London. This was the London Metropolitan Police force, set up by the then Home Secretary, Sir Robert Peel, in 1829.

The London force was what we would recognise now as a "proper" police force. The constables were paid, trained, and given a uniform and a truncheon. Above the constables were the ranks of sergeant, inspector and superintendent. The Peelers or Bobbies as they were called after their founder, proved very successful at controlling crowds in the capital and bringing criminals to justice, so the idea was accepted generally as a good one. Where London led, other towns followed, but not very fast. The change came in Derby in 1835.

In that year, Parliament passed the Municipal Corporations Act, which in fact meant a reorganisation of local government in towns. One result of this was that important towns or boroughs could set up their own police forces, on the lines of the Metropolitan police. The Derby Borough Police started in 1836.

At that time, law and order in Derby was being maintained by six parish constables (parishes in towns had the same system as rural parishes) and ten night watchmen. The watchmen were employed by the town council to patrol the streets at night, calling out the hours, and keeping a watch for any suspicious goings-on. The constables and the watchmen did something to deter and arrest criminals, but they were not very efficient. If there was any serious trouble, as there had been during the Reform Riots in 1831, the normal forces of law and order were powerless. Then the magistrates had to enlist special constables hurriedly and, in the end, call for military help. A few determined arrests at the start of the rioting might have prevented all the later trouble.

The new Borough Police in 1836 consisted of eight police constables, two sergeants and a superintendent. There were also to be five watchmen for night patrol from April 1st to September 30th, and ten from October 1st to March 31st. These watchmen were later recruited into the police force. The Watch Committee of the town council set out its Orders and Regulations in some detail. The superintendent was to be paid £150 a year, and to have a free house next to the Police Office. Sergeants were to have 20 shillings a week for the first year and 21 shillings after that. Constables, or privates as they were called, were to be paid 17 shillings a week for the first year and 18 shillings later.

The wages for constables were rather low, and it was feared that the wrong type of man might come forward to join the police. This had been a very big problem in the London police. So the committee's rules stated clearly

> Sobriety will be most strictly enforced and any constable being intoxicated will be subjected to such fine as the Committee may determine, or to instant discharge, and no constable will be allowed on any pretence while on duty to enter a public house, except in the execution of his duty.

They were also concerned that the police constable should project a good image, and must exercise almost superhuman self-control - and all on 17 shillings a week!

> Neither resentment nor anger is becoming in him, and in proportion as he displays forebearance and coolness will his merit be in the eyes of the public.

Irongate, Derby, about 1860, with three of the new peelers keeping the peace. Derby Central Library, Local Studies Department. *(Photo: Anthony Fisher)*.

His conduct to persons in custody must be temperate and firm; on no occasion must he be irritated or violent, and never use more force than is required to secure the safe custody of persons in his charge.

As well as all this, the constable must always be properly dressed in the correct uniform, and the committee made the point that the uniform must be returned when a constable leaves the service.

However, unlike the old parish constable, the new police constable was given some indication of his rights. Whether this was altogether reassuring to a new recruit is another matter!

The constable may arrest one whom he has just cause to suspect to be about to commit an illegal act. Thus, when a drunken person or a man in a violent passion threatens the life of another, the constable should interfere and arrest him.

The Derby Borough Police force proved itself to be as useful to the town as the Metropolitan Police had proved in London, and it continued to expand as the population of the town grew. Meanwhile, the county outside Derby was policed, if that is the right word, by the old parish constable system. This was becoming increasingly ineffective as time went on.

A most unconstitutional force

In 1839 an Act was passed which allowed each county to set up a new-style police force, if it wished. At that time, of course, there were no County Councils, so the decision was up to the J. P.s for each county. The Derbyshire J. P.s meeting in Quarter Sessions on Friday, 1st November 1839 decided to appoint a committee to consider the question in more detail and to hear the opinions of the general public. These were not late in coming; in fact, petitions against a county police force had been organised even before the J. P.s met. Some opinions sent in, however, mentioned the advantages of a county police, which would, for example, prevent

many depredations from being committed by the numerous vagrants who are constantly traversing the county, for the double purpose of begging and stealing, and have frequent recourse to intimidation where they find premises and property left to the care of females remote from neighbours.

The committee of J. P.s, aware of opposition to a county force, considered experimenting with police in some areas of Derbyshire only, for a start, but then decided it should be everywhere in the county or nowhere. If some parts of Derbyshire were protected by police

> the effect would be greatly to increase the insecurity of property in the unprotected parts. For the same reason, the adoption of the Act in the adjoining counties of Nottingham, Leicester and Stafford makes the adoption of it here merely a question of time.

In other words, the presence of an efficient police force in neighbouring counties would result in all their rogues and criminals congregating in Derbyshire.

The committee therefore recommended that Derbyshire should have a county police force of 60 constables with six superintendents and one Chief Constable. The J. P.s worked out the following cost sheet

1 Chief Constable	£300
6 Superintendents £75 plus clothing	£486
60 Constables 18 shillings per week	£2808
Clothing for 60 @ £6	£360
Total annual cost	£3954

The committee noted that the force would amount to one policeman to about 3,000 people, which was three time less than the ratio permitted by Act of Parliament. Nottinghamshire and Leicestershire were going ahead with similar schemes. The cost would be met by increasing rates by a little over 1 penny in the pound. The J. P.s even suggested that the real cost would be less because the expense of trials, prosecutions and dealing with prisoners would be reduced.

But petitions against having a County police force poured in. Most of these simply objected on the grounds of cost but some went into more detailed arguments. Fifteen parishes in the Hundred of High Peak sent a joint petition explaining why they simply did not need police

> with the exception of two or three cotton mills, a paper mill and some stone quarries, there is little or nothing but agricultural pursuits.....
> ... religious and moral duties generally prevail, crime is rarely committed, the rights of persons and property are as secure here as in any part of her Majesty's dominions.

Police Uniforms in Derbyshire Police Museum. Left: 1839 uniform of frock-coat, white trousers and top hat. Right: 1851 uniform. *(Photo: Anthony Fisher)*.

The petition from Breadsall similarly declared how quiet and peaceful the parish was

> there being but two seasons in the year, viz., the Annual Wakes, and Whitsuntide, when any disturbances ever occur, and that the constable of the parish has always been found sufficient to restore order.

The people of Breadsall, however, went on to express a fear which other people felt as well - the fear that a paid, uniformed police would terrorise and spy on ordinary citizens. The petition declared that the rural police would be

> a most unconstitutional force in our free country; a step to the introduction of that wretched system of espionage and tyranny which prevails in the police departments on the Continent.

In the face of such objections and fears, the Derbyshire J. P.s withdrew their plans, and the old system of parish constables continued for another seventeen years.

Oil and wick for use of lanterns

The County police force was established in the end as a result of an Act of Parliament passed in 1856. This new Act compelled each county to establish a regular police force, so this time there could be no arguments and no delay. The Derbyshire J. P.s went ahead and at the Quarter Sessions in December 1857 they had the pleasure of hearing their chairman read a letter from the Home Secretary, saying

> Your Police has been maintained in a state of efficiency in point of numbers and discipline since its establishment in the terms of the 16th Section of Statute 19 and 20 Victoria.

By 1860, the total strength was 156. Of these, 101 were constables, 29 were sergeants or acting sergeants, and there were two detectives. The numbers increased gradually over the following years and people came to accept the uniformed peace-keepers in their towns and villages.

Not only did the people of Derbyshire accept the new police without too much grumbling, but within twenty years villages without a policeman were asking for one, as the following petition shows.

Subdivision of _Ashford_				Journal of _Constable Britton Simpson No 2 L_ from 6 a.m., to 6 a.m.				

Date. 1859	Hour of going on duty.		Hour of coming off duty.		Names of Places visited.	Hour when visited.		Remarks of Constable as to occurrences.	Superintend Remarks.
	a.m.	p.m.	a.m.	p.m.		a.m.	p.m.		
28 Saturday	10	"	"	2½	Ashford	10	"	Visited the above Places	
"	"	"	"	"	Sheldon	11	"	remained ½ an hour	
"	"	"	"	"	Ashford Tole Gate	12	"	the Conference met Constable	
"	"	"	"	"	Churchdale	"	1	No 7 9 at Ashford Tole Gate	
"	"	"	"	"	Wormhill	"	½	at 12.45. no report	
"	"	"	"	"	Ashford	"	2½	Patrolled home 4½ hours	
"	"	7½	2	"	Ashford	"	7½	Visited the Above Places	
"	"	"	"	"	Bakewell	"	8	Proceeded to Bakewell	
"	"	"	"	"	Ashford	"	8½	with the Special Charges	
"	"	"	"	"	Taddington	"	10½	Met Supt Ruskat R Pn	
"	"	"	"	"	Priestcliff	"	11 5	Proceeded to Taddington	
"	"	"	"	"	Ashford	2	"	Patrolled the Village 5	
"	"	"	"	"		"	"	returned to Ashford and	
"	"	"	"	"		"	"	found many Drunk	
"	"	"	"	"		"	"	And Disorderly people	
"	"	"	"	"		"	"	Patrolled home 6½ hours	
29 Sunday	9	"	"	1	Ashford	9	"	Visited the Public Houses at	
"	"	"	"	"	Sheldon	"	"	Sheldon and Ashford And	
"	"	"	"	"	Hadstone	10½	"	Hassop Little Longstone	
"	"	"	"	"	Little Longstone	11	"	Great Longstone Patrolled	

A page from the Journal of Constable Milton Simpson, May 1859. Derbyshire Police Museum. *(Photo: Anthony Fisher).*

Stocks discovered at Church Farm, Denby. No one seems to know when they were made or last used. (The use of stocks as a punishment has never been made illegal). The holes for the legs are unusually large, and there are other suspect features. The publisher would welcome any information or solution to the mystery. *(Photo: David Mitchell).*

Police lock-up at Alfreton. Before the days of fast motor transport such buildings were used for short-stay prisoners, generally overnight. Notice the huge roof-slabs. *(Photo: David Mitchell).*

The Humble Petition of the undersigned inhabitants of Dethick, Lea and Holloway. Whereas the said township contained in the year 1871, a population of nearly 1000 souls . . . . and whereas the hosiery mills, the lead smelting works and the quarries . . . employ a great number of people . . . . and whereas the residents and employees aforesaid are liable and subject to the visits of numerous vagrants who are a source of annoyance and sometimes of alarm, and whereas there is no resident Police Constable nearer than Crich or Cromford

Your petitioners pray that . . . . a Police Constable be permanently stationed at Holloway.

And in this case, the petitioners were successful, as the note at the end of it shows.

Approved 16 Sept. 1879 by Wirksworth Petty Sessions Justices.

So the new Derbyshire Police were now wholeheartedly accepted and instead of the 18th century unpaid, untrained parish constable, law and order in the county now depended on the Victorian village policeman, the system which lasted until the comparatively recent arrival of the Panda car.

How Victorian the new system was is illustrated by the allowances provided for by the J. P.s in their Quarter Sessions in April 1858. Policemen covered their beats on foot.

Boot money for sergeants and constables . . . 2 shillings per month

Boot money for superintendents . . . 2 shillings and sixpence per month

Superintendents also had coach house stabling allowance. . . 10 shillings per month.

Travel over long distances was by rail.

Superintendent travelling by railway on duty. . . 2 pence per mile

Sergeants and constables travelling by railway on duty. . . 1 penny per mile

Fifteen hundredweight of coal was allowed for lock-up houses in the winter months and ten hundredweight in summer. And for policemen on night duty the allowance was

Oil and wick for use of lanterns. . . eight pence per man per month

CHAPTER FIVE

Transportation and other punishments

To be whipped at Derby

Margaret Blood, wife of **Thomas Blood of Horsley,** found guilty of stealing a parcel of wool, is ordered to be whipped at Derby in the usual manner.

How many times that sentence was recorded at Derbyshire Quarter Sessions court! And in courts all over the country too in the 18th century. The usual manner meant according to the time-worn phrase, "until her back be bloody". There was no set number of lashes for criminals as there was in cases of flogging in the Army and the Royal Navy. The phrase meant simply that the whipping went on until the victim's back was bleeding freely. The whipping was done in public, normally in the market place in Derby or another large town, and was sure to attract a crowd of spectators, to whom it was meant to be a warning. As we see in this case, there was no special leniency shown to women, nor was there to children. Public whipping was the commonest punishment for minor crimes.

Even that was a softer punishment than some which the 18th century inherited from earlier times. These included maiming an offender by cutting off, or cropping the ears, and branding or "burning in the hand". These barbaric penalties were no longer given by the end of the

49

18th century, and even public whipping became less common, although flogging was still practised in the comparative privacy of the prison.

The stocks and the pillory were used as punishments right through the 18th century, but were also less and less used in the early 19th century. The intention of this punishment was to make the criminal known to the public, who could then avoid having dealings with him or her in the future. The authorities knew, of course, that the onlookers would throw garbage and mud, or even stones at the criminal. Even though this was not in fact allowed by law, the constables turned a blind eye to it. A difficulty for the legal authorities was that while one person might be very badly treated and even injured in the pillory, a popular criminal who had the sympathy of the crowd suffered only slight inconvenience.

A news item in the Derby Mercury on October 17, 1776, tells of a man pilloried at Mansfield for fraud.

> As soon as he was mounted on the pillory he told the populace that if they pelted him he would prosecute them. This had its effect for about three quarters of an hour, when they could refrain no longer, but accordingly pelted him with filth, etc., in a pretty severe manner.

Fines and imprisonment were used as punishments in the 18th century, but not to the same extent as at the present day. For fining to be effective, of course, the criminal has to have enough money to pay the fine; otherwise there must be an alternative punishment such as imprisonment. Prisons in the 18th century were generally very small and, apart from the Houses of Correction, were not regarded as places of punishment in themselves. People were kept in prison awaiting trial or until their actual punishment was given; and debtors were kept in prison until their debts were paid, but detention in these cases was not regarded as a punishment - however much it might seem so to the unfortunate prisoner!

The standard punishments for what were regarded as serious crimes were hanging and transportation. The latter was a common punishment in itself as well as being used as a substitute for the death penalty if the court was feeling merciful. What the 18th century considered serious crimes differed from our present view. Instead of saying that felonies carried the death penalty, it would be more accurate to say that any crime to which the death penalty was attached was a felony. We might nowadays accept that, in the past at least, murder would merit a sentence of death, but in fact in the early 19th century there were over two hundred separate offences for which death was the prescribed punishment. Parliament believed that Britain was suffering from a crime wave in the 18th century, and the simplest answer was to impose the death penalty more freely, increasing the number of capital crimes from fifty to two hundred. These included theft, robbery, arson, forgery, sending threatening letters and smashing industrial machinery. The intentions of Parliament were often frustrated, however, by the courts, because juries would prefer to declare an obvious offender not guilty than to send him or her to the gallows for a crime which in their opinion did not deserve death.

Hanged by the neck

For those who were sentenced to death the prospect was unenviable. After receiving sentence, there was usually a delay of a few weeks. During that time the condemned person was usually kept fettered, and apart from other prisoners. The waiting was made worse in some cases by the hope that a pardon would be granted, or the death sentence changed to transportation. This hope tantalised the four arsonists, mentioned in Chapter Two, who were eventually hanged, in 1817.

In the early 18th century hangings in Derby were carried out in a way somewhat reminiscent of the lynching practised in the Wild West of America, using a gallows - a stout wooden beam for lack of a convenient tree - and a cart, The gallows was set up in the Market Place or other convenient open space. There is quite a detailed account of the hanging of Matthew Cocklane, whom we met in Chapter Two, in the Derby Mercury, March 28, 1776.

> He was taken out of the Gaol and put into the Cart about a quarter past eleven o'clock. On his way to the gallows a person (who is said to be a Preacher amongst the Methodists) got into the Cart and read to him all the way. When he arrived at the tree he got out of the Cart and the Rev. Mr. Henry prayed by him for some time. The Under-Sheriff indulged him nearly an hour and a half in his devotion, after which he seemed quite composed, got into the Cart, fixed the Rope and assisted the executioner in pulling the cap over his face; all this he did with the greatest resolution. At half past one the Cart was drawn away which launched him into a boundless eternity.

The same features of the process of execution appear in the report of the hanging of Mary Dilkes in Derby, in 1754.

> Last Saturday, betwixt Twelve and One o'clock, **Mary Dilkes** was, (pursuant to her sentence at the late Assizes, for the Murder of a Bastard Child) carried in a cart from the Gaoler's House to the usual place of Execution, where, after spending some time in Devotion, being assisted therein by a Clergyman, she was executed, amidst a vast number of Spectators.

The report continues, mentioning the usual fate of the body of an executed criminal.

> After which her Body was taken down, and being put again into the Cart, was brought to the County Hall for Dissection.

The following week, the Derby Mercury confirmed this gruesome piece of information.

> Last week the Body of Mary Dilkes was dissected; and the Parts explained to the young Gentlemen of the Faculty by Mr. Meynell, Surgeon, of this place.

An alternative treatment was carried out in the case of Matthew Cocklane. According to the Derby Mercury:

> Cocklane's body is now hung in chains in a place called Bradshaw Hay, adjoining to this Town. He was to have been dissected but several gentlemen having applied to the Judge desiring he might be hung up, an Order for that purpose arrived about six o'clock on Thursday morning.

This hanging in chains of a criminal's body after execution was done on a gibbet. This was a strong wooden post with a cross piece at the top. The body was tarred, wrapped round with chains or placed in a kind of metal cage, and left hanging for weeks or months as an awful warning to others. This had been the traditional way; giving the body for dissection to increase the knowledge of medical students was an 18th century improvement.

The crowd at a hanging liked to have the drama heightened by some unusual incident, and they liked the convicted person to behave well. Either a sincere repentance or a devil-may-care appearance would do nicely. The spectators did not enjoy a dull execution.

Matthew Cocklane scored highly with a full confession and an interesting "Life, Tryal, Behaviour, Confession and Last Dying Words". Mary Dilkes gave so many different accounts of her life and the crime she had committed that the Derby Mercury reported, with obvious disappointment the publishing what is commonly called a Confession, etc., on such Occasions, could not have given that Satisfaction to the Public as might have been expected from one in her unhappy Circumstances; 'twas therefore thought most prudent to decline publishing any Thing of that Kind.

The four arsonists put up a very poor show indeed, in 1817.

They were brought out upon the scaffold about a quarter before one o'clock and seemed but little affected by the sad solemnities by which they were surrounded.

They spoke familiarly to their acquaintances who came to witness their tragical end. The drop fell from under them about five minutes after one o'clock, and they seemed to die without a struggle.

You may have noticed that by this time, 1817, the old cart and gallows had given way to the more up-to-date platform with a trap-door (the drop) set up right outside the gaol. One can imagine that, for the crowd, this did not have the same appeal as the older method. Especially if the person to be hanged had a certain flair for publicity, the cart gave more scope for entertainment.

A horse thief, George Steel, alias John Pilkington, was hanged in Worcester in 1754. He carried off his last journey in the cart with a great deal of swagger, at one place asking the driver to stop to let him buy a hot mutton pie from a street-vendor, and then deciding that it would not do him much good. Like a true showman, however, he saved the best bit of business to the end. When he arrived at the place of execution, according to the newspaper account, he

. . . . seemed very impatient to be dispatched, and, as soon as the rope was placed round his neck, he threw himself off the cart with a great swing, not waiting for its being drove away.

Some of His Majesty's Plantations

Henry Storer, late of the parish of Wirksworth in the County of Derby, collier, being tried and found guilty of feloniously stealing one coarse linen bag, commonly called a sack, of the value of ten pence, and six pecks of oatmeal therein contained, of the value of three shillings. It is ordered by this court that the said Henry Storer be transported as soon as conveniently may be to some of his Majesty's colonies or plantations in America for seven years to be computed from the time of his conviction.

This sentence recorded in the Court of Quarter Sessions in January 1764 is typical of thousands during the 18th century. Notice the care with which Henry Storer is charged with stealing not only the oatmeal but also the "linen bag, commonly called a sack", and the absence of any specific destination for him. We feel that the J. P.s were only anxious to get him out of England and where exactly he was taken to did not matter very much - anywhere in America would do. The entry in the Derbyshire Quarter Sessions Order Book goes on

> And it is further ordered that **Sir John Every, baronet, Henry Eyre, William Fitzherbert and John Gisborne,** Esquires, Justices of the Peace for this County, or any two of them be appointed to contract with any person or persons for the transportation of the said Henry Storer.

Mostly when we think of transportation, we imagine it to have been very highly organised and supervised. We think of convict ships sailing for Australia, with armed guards aboard, everything provided for by the State. That was true of 19th century transportation. In the 18th century, as we see, the destination was America, and instead of a properly fitted-out convict ship, two J. P.s are appointed to find someone who will take on the job of shipping Henry Storer out to the colonies. If we follow the fortunes of another couple of transported felons through the records in the Derbyshire archives, we shall find out how the arrangements worked.

Our heroes, if that is the best word for them, are Joseph Smallwood and John Tugby, both labourers, who lived at Willington. They first appear in information laid before the local J. P. on 3rd January 1770, by George Doncaster. Doncaster was a clerk of William Greaves of Ingleby who owned Willington Wharf. Doncaster reported to the J.P.

> On Saturday morning last, he found two crates of pots at Willington Wharf, broke open, and there was two or three dozen of earthen plates stolen out of one of the said crates, and above two dozen earthen dishes stolen out of the other crate, which dishes and plates are the property of Mr. Thomas Bacchus of Shelton in Staffordshire. He hath cause to suspect Joseph Smallwood and John Tugby, labourers, to have stolen the same.

Off goes the parish constable to arrest the pair, and haul them before the J. P. Smallwood makes a full confession, recorded by the clerk.

Know all Men by these Presents that I Jonathan Forward Sydenham of the City of London Merchant am held and firmly bound to Godfrey Heathcote Gentleman Clerk of the Peace for the County of Derby in One hundred Pounds of good and lawfull money of Great Britain to be paid to the said Godfrey Heathcote or his certain Attorney Executors or Administrators for the true payment whereof I bind myself my Heirs Executors and Administrators firmly by these Presents Sealed with my Seal Dated this second day of April in the Year of our Lord One thousand seven hundred and sixty eight ———

Whereas Charles Dethick and William Russell now remaining in his Majesty's Gaol for the County of Derby to be transported to some of his Majesty's Colonies or Plantations in America for fourteen Years pursuant to an order ... at the last General Delivery of the Gaol for the County of Derby to be accounted from the time of their conviction And whereas the said Jonathan Forward Sydenham hath agreed with two of his Majesty's Justices of the Peace for the said County of Derby for the transportation of the said Charles Dethick and William Russell The Condition therefore of the above written Obligation is such that if the above bounden Jonathan Forward Sydenham his Heirs Executors Administrators or Assigns do and shall so soon as conveniently may be transport and convey the said Charles Dethick and William Russell to some of his Majesty's Colonys or Plantations in America there to remain according to the ... recited Order and if the said Jonathan Forward Sydenham shall procure an authentic Certificate from the chief Governor or Custom house officers of the place of Landing the ... Charles Dethick and William Russell (Death and Casualty of the Sea excepted) and deliver the same to the said Godfrey Heathcote his Successors or Assigns within thirteen Months after the Delivery of these and if the ... Charles Dethick and William Russell shall not be suffered to return to any part of Great Britain or Ireland within the term aforesaid by the consent or neglect of the said Jonathan Forward Sydenham his Heirs or Assigns Then this obligation to be void otherwise to be and remain in full force and virtue ———

Sealed and delivered (being first duly stampt) in the presence of

Henry Coulson
Rich.d Cooper

Jonathan Forward Sydenham agrees with the County authorities to transport Charles Dethick and William Russel to "some of His Majesty's Colonys or Plantations in America", April 1768. Derbyshire County Record Office. (Photo: Anthony Fisher).

On Saturday night last, about eight o'clock, he, in company with one John Tugby did upon Mr. Greaves' Wharf at Willington in this County, cut open one crate and took thereout about two dozen of cream colour'd plates and about one dozen of cream colour'd small dishes and laid them under a hedge bottom all that night. On Sunday morning about eight or nine o'clock they took the plates and dishes and carried them to one Thomas Taylor, a publican at Stanton by Swarkestone Bridge, and sold them to two men who were in his house, a-drinking. He says John Tugby sold the plates and dishes, but he cannot say for how much money, for that John Tugby gave him only one shilling.

Obviously Joseph Smallwood was by now feeling very resentful about the whole affair. He should never have gone along with John Tugby in the first place. All he had got for it was one shilling, which he had probably spent straight away in the public house at Stanton-by-Bridge. And now they were both in serious trouble. He must have been very depressed as he clumsily took the quill pen and made his cross at the bottom of the confession where the clerk had written his name. Then it was off to the County Gaol in Derby for Smallwood and Tugby, until the next Quarter Sessions, where they were tried and, of course found guilty. The case is recorded as follows.

> **Joseph Smallwood and John Tugby** both late of **Willington** in this County, labourers, being indicted and arraigned for feloniously stealing and carrying away two dozen of earthen plates of the value of five shillings . . . and pleading guilty . . . . It is ordered by this Court that the said Joseph Smallwood and John Tugby be transported as soon as conveniently may be, to some of his Majesty's colonies or plantations in America for the term of seven years.

After appearing and being sentenced at Quarter Sessions, Smallwood and Tugby were taken back to gaol to await transportation. Meanwhile, the J. P.s were busy arranging for someone to take them. This someone turns out to be a London merchant by the name of Jonathan Forward Sydenham.

We find an agreement drawn up and signed by him and Sir John Every and John Gisborne, J. P.s, referring to the trial and sentence, and continuing

> . . . . that the said Joseph Smallwood and John Tugby be delivered by Blythe Simpson, Keeper of His Majesty's Jail for the said County unto the said Jonathan Forward Sydenham on or before the first day of November next.

The J. P.s also undertake

> at the time of the delivery of the said convicts to pay the sum of four guineas unto the said Jonathan Forward Sydenham.

The same firm had been in this business of dealing with the transportation of Derbyshire convicts for two or three generations. In 1725, the Clerk of the Peace had an offer from a London merchant, Jonathan Forward, as follows

> I have received a letter from Mr. Edward Cheney advising that there was two persons in the gaol at Derby as lyes for Transportation . . . . . I shall have a ship ready to take in felons in about six weeks time and if you are willing to give me four pounds per head when delivered to me in London clear of all charges, I shall be willing to take them, it's what I have from all other countys. Your answer to this will be acceptable and then I shall write you what day I would have them sent.
>
> I am
>
> Your humble servant
>
> Jonathan Forward

No doubt this Jonathan Forward gave satisfaction, as Derbyshire was still dealing with his successor in 1770, as we have seen.

When the final date was arranged between the Keeper of the Gaol, Blythe Simpson, and Jonathan Forward Sydenham, Smallwood and Tugby had to be taken to the port from which the ship was to sail. This journey, and indeed the whole business of arranging the transfer of the prisoners from Derby to London or Liverpool was a complicated and costly affair. We can see this from an expenses account which survives, sent in to the J. P.s by the gaoler in Derby after such a trip in 1751. It is headed

> John Greatorex Account
>
> A computed charge of the prisoners to be transported

First there are the preliminary arrangements to be made. These items include

A messenger to Leverpoole, his horse hire 5 days @ 2 shillings per day	0 - 10 - 0
My man spent in the journey	14 - 8
I have 4 letters from London cost	1 - 6

There is also a separate account sent to him from his brother in London. It must have been very useful to have a reliable agent there, who could see people personally. His brother's bill consists of

3 post letters @ 5d a peace	1 - 3
spent in going 4 times waiting on Mr. Forward	5 - 0

Then for the actual journey to "Leverpoole" he has to have a vehicle large enough to carry his prisoners - there are eleven of them altogether. Even though the convicts are chained, he needs guards in case they try to get away, perhaps when staying overnight on the journey. It takes four days to get to Liverpool. He and his personal servant, and the guards and the convicts all have to be lodged and fed. He hires a large covered waggon and that and the other items cost as follows.

Agreed with John Goodman if the Justices of the Peace think fitt for his Waggin 8 days	7 - 0 - 0
Charge of 11 prisoners 4 days at 18d a day apeace	3 - 4 - 0
2 horse hire 8 day apeace	1 - 4 - 0
4 men at 2 - 6 a day apeace for 8 day	4 - 0 - 0
Myself and horse charges 8 day at 5 shillings per day	2 - 0 - 0
My man and horse charges 8 days at 3 - 6 per day	1 - 8 - 0
By expenses upon the road, servants and gards	10 - 0

The total amount came to twenty pounds, eighteen shillings and five pence.

What Joseph Smallwood and John Tugby must have thought of such a journey we can only guess. It must have been very strange to them, and uncomfortable, but probably a pleasant change from being confined in jail in Derby. As the waggon lumbered through Liverpool and down to the quayside where their ship was waiting they had their first sight and smell of the sea, which was alarming for two men who had spent their whole lives as labourers in Derbyshire.

They were then handed over to the master of the ship, who signed for them, and sent them below decks. They were kept locked up until the ship sailed. Occasionally a daring, or lucky, man might escape, as John Carradine, a prisoner from Derby Gaol, did in 1747.

We have a current report that Carradine, who was lately sent from this Gaol to London with three other Persons, in order to be transported, and was actually put on board a Ship for that purpose, has made his escape by swimming to Shore, and that he has since been seen in the Country.

Once the ship set out to sea an escape like that was impossible, and the convicts were usually free to wander about the ship as they pleased, even helping with some fo the seamen's tasks if they could. If the ship called in at an Irish port, as they often did before the Atlantic crossing, the transports would be closely guarded by some of the crew.

After a voyage of about six weeks, the ship arrived at its destination, one of the British colonies in America or an island in the West Indies. Smallwood and Tugby were then hired out as bondservants to work the time of their sentence, for their keep, little better than slaves. Well educated, or skilled men and women who were transported, often were lucky to get a position where they would be valued and treated well, but in the case of illiterate labourers like Smallwood and Tugby, this was unlikely.

The master of the ship was given a certificate by the colonial authorities and this was returned to the Derbyshire J. P.s to show that the process was completed. The certificate naming Smallwood and Tugby no longer exists. It would have read like the following, which mentions another five Derbyshire men, who ended up in the small West Indian island of Antigua.

> Antigua, Port of St. John's
>
> These are to certify that John Bird, Commander of the ship Shawe, of Liverpool here arrived from Liverpool the 25th December 1741, hath here put on shore the undermentioned convicts.
>
> **John Hall, John Charlsworth, William Revell, James Orme** and **Joseph Peach** all mentioned in a regular conviction produced to us by the said John Bird dated the 25th August 1741 under the hands of Thomas Gisborne and John Gisborne, Esqrs. two of his Majesty's Justices of the Peace for the county of Derby.

On receiving a certificate like this from the master of the ship on his return to England, the J. P.s could finally write off Joseph Smallwood and John Tugby, not that they were likely to think of them at all - many other Derbyshire men and women would have gone through the course of justice since those two had first fallen into the hands of the law.

What of Smallwood and Tugby themselves? We can only suppose that their experience in the colonies was like that of many others. When their seven years sentence was up they could, in theory, return to England. Probably they would not, not only because of lack of money, but because the colonies offered wider scope for a new life. Most transports went straight in the colonies and became honest, respectable citizens. The colonies were expanding all the time, trade was increasing, industries were being developed, so there were plenty of jobs to be had. For those who preferred it, there was every chance of starting a small farm, something out of the question for a farm labourer in England, no matter how hardworking he might be.

So in the absence of any evidence to the contrary, we may suppose that Smallwood and Tugby, of Willington, labourers, may in the end have had cause to bless the night they were foolish enough to break open those crates on the wharf and steal the plates and dishes.

IN the Ship *Happy Jennett* of *London*
Joseph Richardson Commander, were Imported the under-mentioned Perfons, Convicts: *being four*
in Number from *Derby (viz.)*

James North
George Lowe
William Pemberton
William Endewon

Port *Annapolis,* }ff. THESE are to Certify, That the
in *Maryland.* above Perfons were here Imported
as aforefaid, the *Tenth* Day of
July paft; and that the
fame Perfons, upon being called over,
did feverally anfwer to their Names.
Given under my Hand and Seal this *tenth* Day of
October in the *twenty fifth* Year of the
Reign of our Sovereign Lord GEORGE the Second,
King of *Great-Britain*, &c. *Annoque Domini* 1751

Jonath Wilson

Document issued in Maryland, then an English colony, certifying the landing of four convicts from Derby. Derbyshire County Record Office. *(Photo: Anthony Fisher).*

CHAPTER SIX

Prisons

The Hulks

Transportation to America had to stop after 1775 when the War of American Independence broke out. The Government of the United States of America obviously did not want Britain unloading her criminals there, so there was a problem. Australia had only just been claimed for Britain following James Cook's exploration of the east coast in 1770, and it was 1787 before the first settlement was made at Botany Bay. Between the end of transportation to America and the beginning of transportation to Australia there was a gap of about twelve years. What was to be done about the hundreds of convicts who could no longer be sentenced to transportation?

To house convicts who would normally have been transported, hulks were used. Hulks were old, unseaworthy men-of-war, fitted up as prisons and moored in the Thames estuary. These continued to be used after 1788 as collection points for convicts being transported to Australia, and some of the Derby rioters of 1831 had the unenviable experience of their dark, damp cages, their sickening food and brutal discipline. The Derby Mercury reported in March 1832

The following convicts were on Tuesday last removed from our County Gaol, to be placed on board the Cumberland Hulk at Chatham, until their several sentences can be further carried into effect; viz. - **John Abell,** to be transported for seven years; **William Atchinson,** seven years; **Thomas Gamble,** seven years; and **George Steeples,** seven years. The two former were found guilty of stealing several articles during the riots in October last.

The hulks were in fact the first prisons to be run by the central government. The other prisons, although called "His Majesty's gaol", were run by the county J. P.s. The first gaol to be built by the government was Millbank Gaol, in 1821. Dartmoor Prison was built to house French prisoners of war and was used for convicts after the Napoleonic Wars ended in 1815. About this time too, Parliament was beginning to think seriously of prison as a place of punishment and reform, where convicts would be subject to some deliberate treatment, and not just kept locked up until they could be transported or hanged.

The House of Correction

This idea, that prison should be a place where a person's character and mental outlook would be permanently changed for the better, was not in fact new. Queen Elizabeth and her advisers had envisaged this in 1601, as part of the Poor Law, a comprehensive scheme to deal with paupers, the disabled, the unemployed, tramps and beggars. A sharp distinction was drawn between those who could not, and those who would not work. The old, the disabled, orphans, and those who could not find work, were to be looked after by the Parish authorities, at home or in the parish workhouse. People who preferred not to work for a living, classed as sturdy beggars, rogues and · vagabonds, · and idle and disorderly persons, were to be put in a House of Correction for a few weeks. They were supposed to be made to work hard at some simple trade, which would, it was hoped, teach them good habits of hard work, and reform their character, as well as being unpleasant enough to make them want to avoid the experience in the future.

Like much Elizabethan reform, central control and direction collapsed as a result of the political revolution of the mid-17th century, and in the 18th century, Houses of Correction were simply used as small local gaols, run by the county J. P.s with very little thought given to their original purpose.

There were five Houses of Correction in Derbyshire; at Derby, Chesterfield, Tideswell, Wirksworth, and Ashbourne. The one in Derby was in fact part of the County Gaol and no distinction was made between people sentenced to the House of Correction in Derby and those lodged in the County Gaol. The state of the others may be seen from a Return sent to the County J. P.s by the Keepers in 1818.

Chesterfield House of Correction was supposed to hold twenty persons, but the Keeper, John Roberts, reported that at one time he had to house twenty-seven. He was allowed, he said,

> Four pence a day from the County where the prisoners have no means of their own, and clothes if wanted - in some cases they are maintained by those at whose instance they have been committed.

The Keepers of Houses of Correction were required to report on the work being done by the inmates, and to estimate its value. The money obtained when the Keeper sold the articles made by the prisoners was supposed to go towards food, clothing, and the upkeep of the House. But John Roberts had to report that no work was done, and explained why!

> The admission of tools and instruments has been thought objectionable, there being no separate workroom to be locked up when the prisoners are not at work, and escapes have heretofore been effected by means of the tools.

William Sheldon, Keeper of the House of Correction at Tideswell, presented a similar report, though it was a much smaller place, only built to hold eight prisoners.

> Value of labour: Not any
>
> Allowances: Two shillings and four pence a week each Prisoner, that have no means of providing for themselves. Allowance of clothing when it becomes necessary. Observations: Twelve out of the number committed in 1818 (fifteen) were and are in custody for a breach of the Game Laws, Bastardy and other misdemeanours.

The so-called Houses of Correction then were obviously not fulfilling their original purpose and were in fact just smaller versions of the larger County and Borough Gaols. They were places of confinement, not of reform, not even of deliberate punishment.

Straw for the Prisoners

> It is ordered by this court that the sum of eight pounds and eight shillings be raised and paid . . . . to Blyth Simpson, Keeper of his Majesty's Gaol . . . . for straw for the prisoners for the year.

So the Derbyshire J. P.s meeting in the Court of Quarter Sessions made provision for the comfort of the prisoners in the County Gaol every year during the 18th century. At the same time, an allowance of bread was made to each felon - the County Bread. Not everyone in the gaol, however, was a convicted felon - some people were waiting to be tried, others were debtors, and these were not entitled to get any food. If they had to ask for the County Bread then they were treated as convicted felons who had fewer privileges. A prisoner who had enough money could, however, buy food, (and drink!) in the gaol. If he had relatives or friends living in Derby they could send food in to him and visit him in the prison once a week, as well as talking to him at the gate every day.

The important thing to remember is that the Derby County Gaol, like others in Britain, was a place of confinement, not punishment. It did not much matter who or what came in to the gaol so long as the prisoners did not get out. What we would consider punishment, like having to sleep on straw on the floor, or having nothing to eat but bread, were not intentional punishments, but merely incidental. Any prisoner could have a proper bed, good food, books, company and other comforts, provided he made the arrangements and could afford them. The new Keeper of the County Gaol, Richard Eaton, objected to this very strongly, in 1821.

> A prisoner having friends (whatever may be his character) may live luxuriously . . . . whilst another, for the same offence, not having friends capable of assisting him, is locked up at sunset and must live upon bread and water.

He also disliked the privilege, for those who did not require the County Bread,

> of having their nearest relative admitted into the prison once a week.
> This, I consider, sir, very improper and what never ought to be allowed.

By that time, conditions in prisons were changing, in Derby Gaol as well as others. The famous prison reformer, John Howard, had been at work, bringing the state of Britain's gaols to the notice of the public and of Parliament. Parliament, as a result, had investigated the matter, and passed two Acts in 1773. The county J. P.s who ran the gaols then had to see that the Acts were carried out. In Derbyshire this resulted in the following orders being made, in 1774.

> It is ordered . . . . that **Mr. John Harrison of Derby,** Surgeon, be appointed Surgeon to the Gaol . . . . and that he be allowed £30 per annum for executing that office, and for finding and providing medicine for the prisoners there.

No fear of Mr. Harrison being over generous in his perscriptions, as the cost came out of his own annual fee!

> It is ordered that the Clerk. . . . do immediately cause advertisements to be inserted in the Derby News papers for any person willing to undertake the making a bath . . . . for preserving the healths of Prisoners in Gaol and preventing the Gaol Distemper.

Gaol distemper, or gaol fever, was a common disease, (generally identified as typhus) which killed prisoners in the 18th century, and on occasions jurymen and judges too, as the germs spread in a crowded courtroom. Soon the J. P.s were pleased to hear that a certain Elisha Simes had submitted an estimate for £98-13-0, "which is the lowest sum that hath been estimated." So the prisoners got their bath.

More concern with the health of the prisoners is shown in a third order.

> That the walls and ceilings of the several cells and wards, both of the Felons and Debtors and also of any other rooms used by the Prisoners in the County Gaol be scraped and whitewashed once in the year, to be regularly washed and kept clean and constantly supplied with fresh air by ventilators, under the care and direction of Mr. Blyth Simpson, Keeper of the said Gaol.

The mention of wards in this order reminds us that in 18th century prisons the inmates were usually kept in large bare rooms, like a hospital ward, rather than in small, individual rooms or cells. And although there was a separate Debtors' side, and a felons' side, within those two broad divisions, men, women and children, those who had been sentenced and those waiting to be tried, all lived together. Separate quarters might be available for those who could pay for the privilege. Cells were used to punish people who broke prison rules, or were too violent to be allowed to mix with other prisoners.

No Beer shall be admitted

The opening of a new County Gaol in 1827 followed soon after Peel's Prisons Act of 1823, which again marked a turning point in ideas and practice. John Howard had already tried to change people's attitude towards prisons. In the early 19th century, Elizabeth Fry continued to appeal to the public to change the whole basis of prisons. Instead of being only a means of keeping people in, prisons now were expected to combine elements of punishment and reform. The emphasis was on hard work, adequate but plain food, improvement in the form of religious services and education for the illiterate, and strictness, whether the prisoners were wealthy or not. Some of the Rules laid down in the 1823 Act, and adopted by the Derbyshire J. P.s illustrate the new ideas.

Prisoners sentenced to hard labour shall . . . work nine hours and a half per day, exclusive of the time allowed for meals . . .

Every Prisoner maintained at the expense of the County shall be allowed daily

of good Wheaten Bread . . . . .24 ounces

Potatoes . . . . .16 ounces

Oatmeal . . . . 4 ounces

Salt . . . . ¼ of an ounce

The visiting Justices shall superintend and direct the instruction of the Prisoners in reading and writing . . . .

Prayers . . . . shall be read every morning at nine o'clock by the Chaplain or the Keeper.

No Prisoner who is confined under the sentence of any Court . . . . shall receive any food, clothing, or necessaries, other than the Gaol allowance . . . .

No tap shall be kept in the Prison; nor shall Spirituous Liquors, or Wine of any kind, Cider, or Perry be admitted for the use of any of the Prisoners therein under any pretence whatever . . . .

Prisoners who do not take the County allowance shall not be permitted . . . . more than one pint of Beer . . . . per day

No Beer shall be admitted into the Prison, except between the hours of twelve and one on weekdays, and between two and half-past two on Sundays, Christmas-day, and Good Friday.

No Gaming shall be permitted in the Prison and the Keeper shall seize and destroy all Cards, Dice or other Instruments of Gaming.

Some of the old practices by which prisoners were completely at the mercy of the governor, the turnkeys and other prisoners, were also stopped after 1823.

No money, under the name of Garnish, shall be taken from any Prisoner, on his or her entrance to the Prison, under any pretence whatever.

The Keeper . . . . shall not, nor shall any Officer of the Prison, sell. . . . any article to any Prisoner.

The Keeper shall keep a Journal, in which he shall record all punishments inflicted by his authority . . . .

No Prisoner shall be put in Irons by the Keeper except in case of urgent and absolute necessity . . . . and the Keeper shall not continue the use of Irons on any Prisoner longer than four days, without an order in writing from a visiting Justice . . .

Leg-irons, ball-and-chain and small truncheon, in Derbyshire Police Museum. Foot, courtesy of David Mitchell. *(Photo: Anthony Fisher)*.

A scrofulous and feeble subject

Life in the new County Gaol in the early 19th century was probably better, at least for the majority, than it had been during the 18th century; but we can hardly imagine that it was pleasant. For one thing, a new theory came into fashion, which laid great emphasis on solitude and silence, so that prisoners could reflect on their past crimes and resolve to reform. Prisoners were not allowed to talk to each other when at work or at exercise, and they spent a great deal of time in their cells. The severity of this policy of isolation varied rather from prison to prison, and Derby Gaol does not seem to have been as strict about it as some. It did, however, cause a problem when it began, because of the heating arrangements. The Surgeon to the Gaol, Douglas Fox, mentions it, in his report of October 1836.

> As the day-rooms are now no longer used in the prison except in the Debtors' Wards, and as the prisoners are therefore obliged, under the separating system to live in the cells, when not at exercise or occupied at the treadwheel, stone-breaking or other outdoor labour, it will be requisite to adopt some plan of warming those cells, otherwise the prisoners would be almost perished during the cold season of the year.

He goes on to say that he had made enquiries about the best way of warming the cells, and suggests that

> steam conveyed through pipes is the plan most approved of in the present day.

The following January, Douglas Fox reports on the extreme cold, nothing having been done by then, of course, about a heating system. His report explains, however, that the prison has temporarily gone back to the old practice of wards, to prevent illness among the prisoners.

> . . . . all inconvenience upon this point has been avoided by permitting the prisoners to sit in the day-rooms, having fires in them, when the weather has been very cold.

By the winter of 1839, the Surgeon is able to remark,

> Much benefit is produced by the new mode of warming and venti-lating the prison, and I believe it is in great measure from those improvements that the prisoners are upon the whole healthy, although the season has been so unusually wet and damp.

Ten years later, Douglas Fox, still Surgeon to the Gaol, could pride himself, in his report, on the excellent health of the prisoners in his charge.

> Indeed at times, during the prevalence of diarrhoea and cholera in Derby there have been no cases existing in the prison. There can, I think, be no doubt this has arisen from the extreme cleanliness and good ventilation of the prison, together with temperance on the part of the inmates.

This is not to say, of course, that all the prisoners were thoroughly healthy. Throughout the 1830's and 1840's Douglas Fox mentions in his reports prisoners who are very ill, or who have died. In April, 1838, there is the case of

> . . . . **Mrs. Davis, or Davil,** an aged debtor, which terminated in death; although this prisoner had every attention and support afforded to her whilst in prison her life was evidently shortened by the depressing effect of long confinement there.

In July, he records the death of,

> . . . . **Goodall,** who was a scrofulous and feeble subject. He was out of health for a considerable time previous to his death. . . .

Interior of cell in Beaumaris Gaol, showing wooden bed, shelf-table, washbasin and toilet arrangement. Mid-nineteenth century. *(Photo: Rhodri Prys Jones).*

In October, he writes

> The two cases requiring observations are those of **Jones,** an elderly and worn out subject. He may continue some time but probably he will not survive long. And **Mangan** who is sinking from pulmonary consumption.

At this time, the average number of prisoners in the gaol on any one day was 110, so there were bound to be some deaths among the old and sick prisoners. More melancholy are the references to suicides. In June, 1837, Douglas Fox mentions

> **Gaunt,** who hanged himself on the 8th of April. He was in good health before he destroyed himself and there had not been any indications that he contemplated committing that act.

In April 1840 he has to report two cases of suicide.

> On the 20th of March **Henry Branderick** hanged himself with a sheet in his cell the morning on which he was to have been tried for a capital offence.

> In the afternoon of the 1st of April **Henry Staples** cut his throat with a razor whilst the barber was preparing to shave him. He was a deserter, daily expecting to be removed to his regiment.

Two days after Henry Staples's suicide, another prisoner was found dead in his cell. He was Thomas Smith, serving three months for assaulting a police officer, and due to be released on 3rd April. That very morning he died in his cell about 4 o'clock. According the the Governor's report.

> The Coroner's inquest assembled at 4 o'clock P.M. on view of the body, and returned their verdict, Died by the visitation of God.

In the new Gaol, prisoners who were fit had to work, according to the 1823 regulations. This was both exercise, pastime and punishment, and in general it had to be simple work, not needing much skill. Breaking stone was a common form of work, and working the tread-wheel, or treadmill, another. The Keeper, or Governor, was always ready to try something different. In 1836 Douglas Fox, the Surgeon, reported on a new form of work at Derby Gaol

> The introduction of the picking of wool assists greatly in arranging how the prisoners shall be employed whose health and infirmities are such as to prevent them being placed on the wheel or at stone breaking.

Treadwheel House, Beaumaris Gaol. Three convicts worked the wheel and three rested, in turn, on the bench just visible behind the railing. *(Photo: Rhodri Prys Jones).*

The food which prisoners got in Derby Gaol varied according to the length of sentence. In 1844, all prisoners kept for three days or less were fed as follows

Breakfast	1 pint oatmeal porridge
Dinner	1 lb bread
Supper	1 pint oatmeal porridge

Men kept between three and fourteen days had the following diet

Breakfast	1 pint oatmeal porridge 6 ozs. bread
Dinner	6 ozs. bread 1 lb potatoes
Supper	1 pint oatmeal porridge 6 ozs. bread

Prisoners of this class employed at hard labour to have in addition one pint of soup per week.

For men kept to hard labour for longer periods there was meat once a week, and soup once a week, and the quantity of porridge went up to one and a half pints, and bread up to 8 ounces. Female prisoners generally were given smaller quantities of food.

Special food was sometimes prescribed by the Surgeon for ill and weak prisoners, as we see from the Governor's Quarterly Accounts. In 1839 these include milk, tea and sugar - the cost per week varying from nil to about a shilling. About the same amount covered the cost of ale and brandy. The quarterly average cost of food per prisoner per week was two shillings and eleven pence. Ten years later more is being spent on milk, tea and sugar - up to 19 shillings, but the number of prisoners is about twice that of 1839 (258 as against 122). Cocoa is now being served at a weekly cost of between £1 - 10 - 0 and £2 - 19 - 0. Wine has been bought only twice in the thirteen weeks, costing eight shillings and four shillings. And the average cost of food per prisoner per week is still two shillings and eleven pence.

NOTES

Derby Gaols

The earliest gaol recorded in Derby was built over Markeaton Brook near the junction of the present Corn Market and St. Peter's Street. This was in use about the middle of the 16th century, at which time the Brook was still open. It continued in use until 1756. William Hutton, writing a History of Derby in 1791, mentioned how, in 1610, three prisoners were drowned when the brook suddenly flooded one night, and he gave as his opinion, "A worse situation could not have been chosen." He went on to write much more enthusiastically of the gaol which replaced it

> . . . . an elegant prison upon Nun's-green (Friargate) in 1756. Here the culprit enjoys light, air and water. . . . The town has the credit of a handsome and suitable edifice; the Duke of Devonshire the pleasure of contributing £400 towards the erection; and the traveller is delighted with the object.

This building occupied numbers 47 to 51 Friargate, where the Howard Hotel (and the phototypesetters for this book Prior to Print!) now stands. It was used as Derby Borough Gaol from 1827 up to 1840, after which date borough prisoners were kept, by arrangement, in the county gaol.

The new County Gaol in Vernon Street was built in 1827, and the Society for the Improvement of Prison Discipline gave its opinion that it was, "of the best plan and construction in the United Kingdom." In accordance with the latest ideas and the rules laid down in Sir Robert Peel's Prisons Act, 1823, it had separate sections for debtors, felons, and people awaiting trial, each section being subdivided into male and female wards. There were also more individual cells.

This prison was used up to 1916 and was sold and demolished in 1929, except for the imposing front entrance. The site is now used as the greyhound racing track.

Escapes

Derby gaols in the 18th century do not seem to have been very secure. In March 1747 the Derby Mercury reported

> Last Saturday Night, the Felons confin'd in the County Gaol, made an attempt to escape having made a large Hole through the Prison Wall into the Street for that Purpose; but it's said, that disputing who should go out first they were overheard, and thereby luckily prevented.

In 1754 the following notice appeared in the Derby Mercury

> Broke out of the County Gaol at DERBY, on Tuesday morning about Three o'clock the 29th of this Instant October, by letting himself off the Leads of the said Gaol by a Rope, one **Cordell Drew,** debtor, comes from Worksop in Nottinghamshire, and has Part of some Mines at Crosley Head near Ashford in Derbyshire:

> The said **Drew** is a short, thick-set Man about Fifty or Sixty Years of Age, with a curl'd bushy Grey Head of Hair, if not cut off, and pretends to know a deal about Mining and may be discovered by his talking very thick. Whoever can approach him so that he may be brought to the Gaol at Derby aforesaid shall receive Five Guineas Reward, of John Greatorex Goaler.

A much more striking figure appears in another escape, of 1755

> Made her escape from the Gaol at Derby on Friday the 21st of February, one **Anne Williamson,** alias **Sparrow,** a handsome faced young woman, about 24 years of age, with dark brown hazzel eyes and looks very sharp, light silver-coloured hair which parts in the middle of her forehead, and about 5 feet five inches high. Had on when she escaped, a dark brown gown, a black turn'd hat, Black

Cell doors in the County Gaol, Vernon Street before demolition. Notice the hatches. *(Photo: Derbyshire Police Museum)*.

quilted petticoat, Pink colour'd stockings, a pair of large silver buckles and a gold ring on one of her fingers, with a long Red Cloak that reach'd below her hips; she talks the Yorkshire Dialect, and belongs to a notorious gang of GAMBLERS; her Father and Mother and another person are now in Leicester Gaol in order to take their tryals at the next Assizes there for stealing Great Coats at Melton fair. Whoever therefore will apprehend and secure the said Anne Williamson, in any of his Majesty's gaols in England, and give notice to John Greatorex, Gaoler at Derby, shall receive Ten Guineas Reward.

The new gaol of 1756 appears to have been much better at keeping people in, but not keeping them out! This was the building the Derby rioters broke into in 1831, using a lamp post as a battering ram.

Sources

Most of the information used in this book comes from two sources: the Derbyshire County Record Office, and the Local Studies Department of Derby Central Library. I am grateful for permission to quote material from these, and am indebted to Miss Joan Sinar, County Archivist, and to Mrs. Anne Mellors of the Local Studies Department, and their respective staffs for their interest and help.

In the main, the sources of criminal cases are informations and complaints laid before the J.P. and the examination of suspects, all held in the County Archives. Reference to criminal cases and orders relating to the County Gaol are to be found in the Quarter Sessions Order Books. The Archives also have a collection of letters, reports and other documents concerning the Gaol.

The Local Studies Department of Derby Central Library has a complete set of the Derby Mercury, which was the local weekly newspaper in the 18th century. These volumes contain reports on criminal incidents, trials and punishments. There is also a set of documents relating to the borough police, as well as many other miscellaneous items.

Beaumaris Gaol

Beaumaris Gaol was built in 1829, two years later than the new County Gaol for Derbyshire in Vernon Street. It was altered and enlarged in 1867, but it was closed by the Prison Commissioners in 1878, along with many similar small gaols in other parts of Britain. It was used by the local police for some years without being much altered, and it was opened as a prison museum in 1975 by Gwynedd County Council.

It is an excellent example of a small County Gaol, and to visit it gives a vivid and lasting impression of what an early 19th century prison was really like. The cells and workrooms are still as they were over a hundred years ago, and the Gaol is unique in having its treadwheel still in the original position in the prison yard.

Further Reading

Most factual books dealing with crime are confined to the 20th century and late Victorian Period, and relate to London gaols and London criminals, and the Metropolitan Police. There are, however, some studies of specific regional crimes, such as smuggling. A few fairly general books on police and prisons are given below.

D. Ascoli **The Queen's Peace:** The Origins and Development of the Metropolitan Police 1829 - 1979. Hamilton 1979.

G. Playfair **The Punitive Obsession:** An Unvarnished History of the English Prison System. Gollancz. 1971.

A. Babington **The English Bastille:** A History of Newgate Gaol and Prison Conditions in Britain. 1188 - 1902. Macdonald. 1971.

E. J. Burford **In the Clink:** The Story of England's Oldest Prison. New English Library. 1977

The following books use documentary evidence and photographs to focus more closely on particular aspects of crime in the 18th and 19th centuries.

J. Brewer and **An Ungovernable People:** The English and their law in the 17th
J. Styles (Ed). and 18th Centuries. Hutchinson. 1980.

J. J. Tobias **Nineteenth Century Crime:** Prevention and Punishment. David and Charles. 1972.

R. Whitmore **Victorian and Edwardian Crime and Punishment from Old Photographs.** Batsford. 1978.

Finally, a few books with a special interest. The first is written for younger readers, and concerns two famous London magistrates of the 18th century. The second includes a short history of the mounted police.

P. Pringle **Henry and Sir John Fielding:** The Thief Catchers. Dobson Books. 1968.

J. Campbell **Police Horses:** David and Charles. 1967.

C. Chenevix Trench **The Poacher and the Squire:** A History of Poaching and Game Preservation in England. Longman. 1967.

If you have enjoyed reading this book, you may be equally interested in our next publication:

Ancient Wells and Springs of Derbyshire

by Peter Naylor

"to forsake Earth's troubled waters for a pure spring"

Byron "Childe Harold"

Derbyshire is particularly noted for the interest of its many ancient wells and springs — thermal waters, ebbing and flowing wells, or simply springs "of pure water, pouring out of the hillsides."

The author looks at an extensive selection of Derbyshire's natural water sources and describes their history, uses both past and present and the ceremonies and traditions associated with them.

Peter Naylor both lives and works in the Peak District of Derbyshire, of which he is a keen historian. He has already written two books on lead mining and dowsing.

The publishers invite would-be authors of books with a Derbyshire flavour to discuss ideas or submit manuscripts with a view to future publication.